Paul Tillich in Plain English

Stephen D. Morrison

Beloved Publishing • Columbus, Ohio

Copyright © 2025 by Stephen D. Morrison

All rights reserved.

No part of this book may be reproduced in any form or by any electronic or mechanical means, including information storage and retrieval systems, without written permission from the author, except for the use of brief quotations.

Cover design and illustration copyright © 2025 Gordon Whitney.

Print ISBN: 978-1-63174-186-9

eBook ISBN: 978-1-63174-187-6

Beloved Publishing • Columbus, Ohio

Contents

Preface: On the Plain English Series	v
Acknowledgments	ix
Introduction	xi
Biography	1
1. Faith and Doubt	15
Sermon: The Divine Name	35
2. God and Being	39
Sermon: Escape from God	61
Sidebar: The Courage to Be	67
3. Christ and Existence	77
Sermon: You are Accepted	101
Sidebar: Atonement Theories	109
Sidebar: Christology and the Resurrection	115
4. Unambiguous Life	123
Sermon: Nothing Real is Lost or Forgotten	139
Sidebar: The Trinity	143
5. The Method of Correlation	147
Sermon: On Being a Theologian	173
6. Conclusion: What Sort of Theologian is Paul Tillich?	177
Reading Guide	185
Bibliography	187

Preface: On the Plain English Series

It has been five years since the latest book in this series, *James Cone in Plain English* (2020). Before diving into this new volume, which is now the sixth installment,[1] I want to highlight a few personal factors that have changed.

When I began with *Karl Barth in Plain English,* I was upfront about my situation as an "amateur" theologian. This series, as a result, has always been oriented around the goal of introducing major theologians from the perspective of an amateur for other amateurs, that is, *for beginners, by a beginner.* I did not say it at the time, but the idea for this approach came from C. S. Lewis, who once suggested that a seasoned expert is actually *less* equipped to explain a subject to beginners than another beginner because a beginner still remembers what it feels like to be new.[2] An expert who has spent their life studying a subject is further away from the difficulties that confront new learners, while a beginner can guide another

---

1. Previous volumes: *Karl Barth in Plain English* (2017), *T. F. Torrance in Plain English* (2017), *Jürgen Moltmann in Plain English* (2018), *Schleiermacher in Plain English* (2019), *James Cone in Plain English* (2020).
2. He writes in his amateur introduction to the Psalms, "The fellow-pupil can help more than the master because he knows less. The difficulty we want him to explain is one he has recently met. The expert met it so long ago that he has forgotten.... In this book, then, I write as one amateur to another..." C.S. Lewis, *Reflections on the Psalms* (New York: Harvest/HBJ Books, 1958), 1-2.

Preface: On the Plain English Series

beginner because they know the struggle well, since they have only just recently overcome it. That does not mean experts are not still vital for learning something new, but it merely suggests that there is something about remembering what it is like to be new to a subject that can help others on their journey.

That insight inspired me to take on a study of Karl Barth, despite my limitations. Those limitations were, at the time, twofold: First, I had no academic degree to my name—not even a bachelor's degree. When I confessed this deficiency in my first book, some readers thought it meant that I simply lacked a theology degree. But my situation was more extreme than that. I did not have *any* college education to my name. And that remained the case for *every* Plain English book up until this point: I wrote those books with only a high school education and a love for reading. (I did go to a two-year, unaccredited ministry school, but it was miles away from anything remotely academic.) My second limitation was this: I could only read in English, while Barth and many other theologians I would go on to study (Moltmann, Schleiermacher, and now Tillich) wrote most of their work in German.

Both limitations have lifted with this new book (which is largely why it has taken so long between volumes). In the Spring of 2024, I graduated with a master's degree in Systematic Theology from Luther Seminary, and as I write this, I am currently a PhD student at the University of Aberdeen. I can also now read some German, albeit slowly (with the help of a dictionary), and I am actively working toward fluency. So the limitations that previously led to calling myself an "amateur" in my first book have changed significantly.

But I want to emphasize what has *not* changed: the spirit of my overall approach. While I cannot say that I am an amateur in the same way I was in 2017, I still approach this series from the perspective of a *newcomer*. What that means, practically, is that each figure is relatively new to me before I begin my research. Before 2023, I had only read two short works by Tillich, and I mostly read them without an understanding of his overall theology. While working on this book, I read for the first time nearly all of Tillich's works in English (and stumbled my way through a few in German), alongside a selection of secondary studies on Tillich's life and thought. I approached him, in other words, as a *newcomer*, not a specialist.

Preface: On the Plain English Series

Thus, I hope to retain the spirit of this series in two ways: First, to remain a *lover* of theology, which is what the root word for "amateur" means. I have always hoped that these books exuded a kind of joy and wonder, because that is precisely how it felt to write them. And second, to approach my subject as a newcomer. In this book, I hope to explain Tillich's theology as someone who has only recently come to terms with it. I am only a few pages ahead of my readers, and I believe that is a strength of this series. And I hope it will remain so as it continues.

These volumes have been a remarkable blessing to me in many ways. They have functioned almost like a public expression of my private theological education. I learned right alongside my readers. Even now, as I take steps toward scholarly research into the theology of Karl Barth (for my doctoral work), I feel more and more as if I am starting from square one. Or, as Barth eloquently put it so often, I am "beginning again at the beginning." And in that regard, I often wonder if a theologian can ever truly be anything but a "beginner."

While my situation has changed, the spirit and approach I have adopted for these books and my overall goal remain the same. Thus, I can fully affirm what I wrote seven years ago at the beginning of my Barth book, "This book is for beginners, by a beginner, on the theology of Karl Barth…" The only difference now is that I am more conscious of (and confident in) myself as a scholar, and that this book is about Paul Tillich.

My approach to this series

Let me say a few words about my process in writing this series. The first principle I follow when setting out is to adopt a hermeneutic of generosity. To me, this means approaching my subject from a posture that suspends disbelief or critique until some degree of familiarity with their thought emerges. In terms of Tillich, it means prioritizing the most charitable reading possible of his theology before engaging in any sort of criticism.

The way this hermeneutic is applied is through a close reading of Tillich's primary texts, combined with a broad reading of almost all of his published writings and much of the secondary literature about him. In other words, I read broadly (not stressing over every detail) but also deeply (focusing on the main points and carefully examining them). In

Preface: On the Plain English Series

the past, I focused on the main text of each theologian, e.g., *Christian Faith* for Schleiermacher and *Church Dogmatics* for Barth. The same is true for this volume. The text I focused on here was Tillich's *Systematic Theology*, but I read it in close connection with his sermons, history lectures, and other important books. I would call this process a kind of "immersive" reading, wherein I expose myself to as much writing as possible, sometimes as many as fifty books.

This balance aims to achieve both the clarity of precision and the broadness of context. I have also tried to keep Tillich's biography in mind throughout this reading, to further add to the context of his work. No theologian writes in isolation from their situation, and that is certainly the case for Tillich, the great theologian of "correlating" the Christian message with the human situation.

This approach has been, for the most part, the same for each volume in this series. To describe it, I would use words like "immersive," "close," and "charitable." But I would also like to add a third idea—perhaps the most important—*existential passion*.

I have never been a passive observer with these books, but am passionately involved in the material I study. Therefore, my readers need to know that each of these books has changed me, as much as I hope it might change you. Whether it is as simple as changing something you think, challenging a presupposition, providing a new vocabulary for your faith, or helping you write a research paper, I hope this series can be as helpful to you as it has been for me. I knew going into this that these books would only work if they were the type of books I would benefit from, and I would like to think I've been successful in at least helping one person: myself. The theologians I have studied are a rich resource for faith. Ultimately, theology is, for me, an act of intellectual love—of loving the Lord with all my heart, soul, and *mind*. As such, it is in the spirit of devotion and gratitude that I submit to you, *Paul Tillich in Plain English*.

Stephen D. Morrison
Columbus, Ohio
2025

Acknowledgments

This book would not be possible without the help of several people in my life.

First and foremost, I want to thank my dear wife Ketlin, who is a constant source of inspiration, support, and love. I would not be half the man I am today without you.

Second, I am grateful to my former professor at Luther Seminary, Lois Malcolm, who led an independent study on Tillich in the Spring semester of 2023. Much of my interpretation of Tillich is indebted to Dr. Malcolm's careful reading of him, although all blame for any inaccuracies is mine.

Third, I would like to thank Brach Jennings, a close friend and astute theologian whom I am honored to know, and with whom I frequently discussed Tillich. I am thankful for the many conversations and encouragements when I often struggled to "get" Tillich.

Fourth, I would like to thank Gordon Whitney, who is not only a dear friend but also the talented illustrator of my book covers for this series. I am forever grateful for the time you have spent making these books look so cool.

Fifth, I would like to thank Ricky Whitefield, who was gracious enough to read this book in draft form and provide me with helpful feedback and encouragement.

And finally, thanks to you, my readers, for picking up this book. It is such an honor for me that you chose to pick up my little book on Tillich, and I hope it helps you in some way.

I dedicate this book to Lois Malcolm and Brach Jennings, who were instrumental in helping me understand and appreciate Tillich.

Introduction

> My whole theological work has been directed to the interpretation of religious symbols in such a way that the secular man—and we are all secular —can understand and be moved by them.[1]
>
> — Paul Tillich

We are all already secular—that is, modern—people, whether we like to admit it or not. That does not mean the end of religion.[2] But perhaps it means the traditional language of the church no longer speaks to us as it once did. Paul Tillich was a theologian who took this situation seriously. He helped make the Christian message existentially relevant to us today, and his efforts toward that end still resonate despite the decades that have passed.

Still, there is perhaps much that gives us pause about his theology, whether it is Tillich's difficulty, his unorthodox life, or his supposed

---

1. Paul Tillich, *Ultimate Concern,* ed. D. Mackenzie Brown (New York: Harper & Row, 1965), 88.
2. See Tillich's concept of "theonomy," outlined in chapter one, which breaks down the sacred-secular divide. See also Bruce. C. Porter's definition of the secular, "The Sacred and the Secular in the Thought of Paul Tillich" (unpublished thesis, 1971: http://hdl.handle.net/11375/10785), 29.

Introduction

"heresy." But before addressing those issues, we need to ask more positively about the value of his thought. So, why read Paul Tillich?

First, as this quote illustrates, Tillich's approach is deeply existential, meaning he relates theology to real life. You will not encounter a purely speculative theology in Tillich, even though it is often wrapped in academic clothing. The core of his theology is the healing power of New Being, that is, Jesus the Christ. Tillich passionately strives to connect the Christian message to our situation. So, whatever difficulties might exist, Tillich's theology shares a core desire with every great systematic theologian from Augustine to Schleiermacher: to proclaim the gospel of Jesus Christ anew.

Second, at a time when many people in the church have gone through seasons of "deconstruction," where the faith they once knew now feels foreign and strange, Tillich's theology offers a framework that embraces doubt and uncertainty as a friend, not an enemy. Deconstruction has become a popular term for those who have begun questioning previously held beliefs about God, the Bible, and the meaning of salvation. Tillich's theology is a fruitful resource on that quest, not least of all because Tillich was, in his own way, a doubter who found himself justified by grace in spite of doubting. Those who have been ostracized by their church community for questioning their previously held beliefs will find in Tillich a friend who has been there and can comfort them on their journey. He offers us a new vocabulary for speaking about faith that embraces these uncertainties yet goes on courageously.

Finally, Tillich remains relevant because he modeled a timely theology that can still speak today. Tillich's theology is timely to such a degree that it is now somewhat outdated. But that is also what is so compelling about it as a model for rethinking the Christian faith for our situation. The model he developed, if not always the conclusions he reached, is sometimes what makes his work so relevant. He explicitly aimed for a theology "on the boundary," and in that very approach, he left us with a model for how to think theologically.

For these reasons, his work remains worth reading. There may be points where his conclusions are no longer helpful, but that is precisely where we might imagine Tillich wants us—even implores us—to leave him behind. Tillich had no interest in turning anyone into a "Tillichian," and this book is not about toeing the line of proper Tillichian thought.

Introduction

Instead, it is sometimes more focused on the *why* and *how* of Tillich's approach than the *what*, though, of course, the what is necessary to consider if we want to understand the why and how.

Outline

The structure of this book loosely follows Paul Tillich's main work: *Systematic Theology*.[3] Loosely—because I have taken liberties to rearrange some subjects in a way that I think best guides readers into Tillich's theology and offers the most charitable reading. For that reason, my first chapter is not "reason and revelation" (part one of Tillich's system), but instead, we begin with Tillich's unique approach to faith and doubt. This subject is one of the most practically helpful aspects of his theology, but it also introduces several key themes from his work.

From there, I move to Tillich's doctrine of God and his concept of symbols (ST1). In particular, I try to clarify some of the difficulties with Tillich's use of symbolic language and his famous concept of God as the "ground and power of being" or "being-itself." Then I focus on Tillich's doctrine of Christ and New Being (ST2), which is also where I discuss his doctrines of redemption, sin, and the fall. This chapter is easily the most important for understanding Tillich, as Tillich himself suggested. Finally, I discuss Tillich's third volume (ST3) on the ambiguities of life and history, which correlate with his doctrines of the Spirit and eschatology.

After studying the content of Tillich's system, I return (in chapter six) to the beginning and look at his *method*, which he called a "method of correlation." Here, I pull together various threads from the preceding chapters to argue that Tillich's correlation method is a theological expression of his profound commitment to an incarnationally structured theology that is at once christologically centered and soteriologically directed. I know these are technical terms, but I will explain what I mean when I get to that chapter.

I conclude with a brief reflection on a somewhat odd question: "What

---

3. Paul Tillich, *Systematic Theology*, 3 vols. (Chicago: The University of Chicago Press, 1951, 1957, and 1963). Throughout this book, I cite Tillich's *Systematic Theology* within the body of the text with the abbreviation "ST," followed by the volume number. This is intentional. I want to keep in front of my readers the central text of this study, in the hopes that they might be encouraged to read this work for themselves.

Introduction

sort of theologian is Paul Tillich?" I try to answer this in a way that helps us think about his contributions and that expresses how his work might be useful for readers today.

Finally, I've included two types of sub-chapters after each main chapter that should be familiar to readers of my earlier books. The first analyzes relevant passages from Tillich's sermons. Tillich frequently emphasized that to understand his theology, it is vital to read his sermons, so I have tried to pair sermons that relate to the central points of each chapter. Second, I've included several "sidebar" chapters, which are designed to address an interesting or insightful aspect of Tillich's theology that relates to, but does not quite fit, the central theme of each chapter. For example, I discuss in detail Tillich's proposal for reformulating the doctrine of the atonement in the sidebar connected to his christology. Each chapter can be understood without these sidebars, but they give me an opportunity to highlight a specific topic from his work that I find relevant.

I should also mention here that there is not one but several Paul Tillichs—a testament to his life "on the boundary" of various disciplines. This book focuses on Paul Tillich the theologian with occasional comments on Tillich the philosopher of religion. But it mostly ignores Tillich the Schelling scholar, philosopher, ethicist, and religious socialist.

I hope there will be much that inspires and challenges you by looking at Tillich's many contributions. No theologian is without their problems, but at the same time, a theologian of such creativity and systematic power as Tillich deserves not only our attention but also our patience. So while I am aware there are many reasons not to study Tillich, I have found myself compelled by his work and hope that readers will also come to discover that patient efforts at understanding him will be rewarded.

The book ends with a brief reading guide. My goal is *not* to replace your own reading of Tillich. Instead, I am trying to make it easier to read him. And so the book ends with a short discussion of Tillich's books as well as the secondary literature on his theology. It is perhaps the most important chapter because my ultimate aim is that you finish this book with the tools to read Tillich for yourself.

Biography

PAUL JOHANNES OSKAR TILLICH was born on August 20, 1886, and he died on October 22, 1965, at the age of seventy-nine. Tillich lived his life "on the boundary" (his phrase), whether it was between Germany and America, philosophy and theology, or church and society. Tillich possessed the unique ability to thrive in the boundary situations of life and thought, and it led to a distinct outlook that shapes his work. But it also led to misunderstanding and rejection from those who wanted him to be either one thing or the other, either a philosopher or theologian, a Lutheran or a socialist, and so on. But Tillich was convinced, "The boundary is the best place for acquiring knowledge."[1]

Tillich's life can be roughly divided into three periods. First, his pre-war adolescence and service as a war chaplain; second, his post-war career as a professor; third, life in America and later fame. These periods overlap, naturally, but each represents a different personal situation from which Tillich thought and wrote. Tillich's theological and philosophical vision was remarkably consistent from period to period, but there are noteworthy changes in style and approach. For example, Tillich's time in America added a pragmatic and practical element to his work that his German period sometimes lacked.

---

1. Paul Tillich, *On the Boundary* (New York: Charles Scribner's Sons, 1966), 13.

The most complete biography of Tillich to date is Wilhelm and Marion Pauck's *Paul Tillich: His Life & Thought*. Tillich also wrote several autobiographical texts: *On the Boundary, My Search for Absolutes,* the introductions to *The Protestant Era* and *The Interpretation of History,* and an essay written for *The Theology of Paul Tillich* (ed. Kegley and Bretall). In addition, there is Rollo May's personal account, *Paulus,* and Hannah Tillich's somewhat problematic book, *From Time to Time.* All these works were consulted for this brief biography, and readers should refer to them for further information about Tillich's life.

Tillich's life has been the subject of some controversy. Let me say something about it briefly. Part of the controversy is warranted, but there is also a lot of speculation surrounding his life and personal relationships. We should try to walk the fine line between hagiography (biography of a saint) and flippant condemnation. Tillich was neither a saint nor a monster. Readers are free to draw their own conclusions about the implications of Tillich's unorthodox life on his theology, but a hermeneutic of charity means suspending judgment until the main work is understood. In this brief biographical sketch, I will refrain from commenting on the various controversies because they, more often than not, only distract from this book's central goal of understanding him charitably.

1. Pre-war Adolescence and War Chaplaincy

Paul Tillich was the firstborn child of Johannes and Wilhelmina Tillich; he was born in a Prussian village called Starzeddel, which is now Starosiedle, Poland. The village is near Berlin, and Tillich was born in the church parish house where his father was a Lutheran pastor. The Tillich family history traces all the way back to the thirteenth century and includes a rich heritage of Augustinian monks, academic lecturers, theologians, and church ministers, but also musicians and manufacturers. However, Tillich's father was the first Lutheran pastor in the family.

When Tillich was born, he barely survived to see August 21. His father wrote, "Little Paul is still alive but his life is a continuous struggle with death..."[2] It is fitting that Tillich's life began with an immediate

---

2. Wilhelm and Marion Pauck, *Paul Tillich: His Life & Thought, vol. 1* (New York: Harper & Row Publishers, 1976), 1.

threat of death hanging over him, since the perpetual threat of nonbeing upon being (met by the "courage to be") is a recurring theme in his theology. But it was not only his own mortality—Tillich was also profoundly affected by the early death of his mother to cancer in 1903, when Tillich was just seventeen. He later wrote about the ambiguities of finite life under the threat of death, but in light of his personal experiences—not only early in life but also during the two World Wars—his focus on a love that triumphs over death is all the more profound because of this dark context. His existential concept of "the courage to be" is not a shallow affirmation of life but a strength rooted in these personal experiences with the fragility of finite life.

Two years after he was born, the Tillich family moved to Schönfliess, a small medieval town with a variety of old landmarks and churches. When, at the age of eight, he laid eyes on the Baltic Sea, he said it was his first experience with the idea of the infinite. Another central theme for Tillich's theology is the phenomenon of the holy, and this experience of natural wonder, together with Christian symbols, filled his childhood with awe and made a deep impression on him from a young age. Even in adolescence, Tillich had been grasped by what he would later call an "ultimate concern."

Tillich's early years also exposed him to less privileged classmates, which sowed the seeds that would bloom later in life into a passionate defense of religious socialism. He was sympathetic to the poor students in his class. The family later moved to Berlin, where Tillich attended the Friedrich Wilhelm Gymnasium; there, he was exposed to key philosophers like Fichte and Kant.

After gymnasium, Tillich studied theology at the University of Berlin. It was at university that Tillich was exposed to Friedrich Schelling, who became the subject of his two doctoral dissertations and made a deep and lasting impression on his thought. Because of the way the German university system was set up at the time, Tillich was able to take classes at various universities across the country, and so Tillich studied not only in Berlin but also in Tübingen and Halle (where he spent two years). At Halle, Tillich encountered Professor Martin Kähler, who profoundly impacted him. It was from Kähler that Tillich learned that justification by grace through faith is not only for the individual as a sinner but also as a doubter. This idea "brought him immense relief."[3] Tillich also joined the Wingolf society, where he later served as a student leader.

Tillich graduated with a degree in both philosophy and theology. He earned a PhD in philosophy at the University of Breslau in 1910, then in 1911, he passed examinations for a degree of Licentiate of Theology at the University of Halle, which was, at the time, the highest degree conferred in theology (the degree was conferred in January 1912). Tillich was also ordained as a minister of the Evangelical church of the Prussian Union in 1912, and worked as an assistant preacher for two years in a working-class district of Berlin.

The two dissertations Tillich wrote for his degrees were on Friedrich Schelling.[4] He earned his theological degree with a thesis entitled, "Mysticism and Guilt Consciousness in Schelling's Philosophical Development." His PhD was awarded based on a thesis called "The Conception of the History of Religions in Schelling's Positive Philosophy: Its Presuppositions and Principles." That is how, at the young age of twenty-six, Tillich held both a doctorate of philosophy and a licentiate of theology. In 1912, Tillich decided to become a professor, and so he started work on a habilitation thesis, or qualifying thesis, which would earn him the right to teach at the university level. He wrote on "The concept of the supernatural in German theology during the period of the enlightenment" during his time serving as an assistant pastor in Berlin.

In 1914, Tillich married his first wife, Margarethe Wever, who was called Grethi. She was a seductive woman, and many people in Tillich's life disapproved of their marriage. But their engagement was announced in January, and the couple married on September 28, 1914. Almost immediately, on the first of October, Tillich volunteered for military service. The First World War had begun, and it would change Tillich's life and outlook drastically.

Before the war, there was a general mood of naive optimism and patri-

---

3. Ibid., 19.
4. While Tillich certainly learned a lot from Schelling, it would be a mistake to call him a "Schellingian." Tillich's use of philosophy is more fluid, and it is difficult to place him in any one "school." See Andrew O'Neill, *Tillich: A Guide for the Perplexed* (London: T&T Clark, 2008), chapter six, for a discussion of Tillich's use of philosophy; see also the vital intellectual background provided by Christian Danz, *The Theology of Paul Tillich* (Macon, GA: Mercer University Press, 2024), chapters 1-2.

otism. Most of the fighters who enlisted were under the assumption that the war would be over quickly, that it would be a glorious fight, and the Prussians would win easily. That optimism was slowly and painfully demolished as the war progressed with all its horror and brutality. Tillich describes those who signed up for the war, including himself: "most of them shared the popular belief in a nice God who would make everything turn out for the best."[5]

Tillich served as chaplain for the Fourth Artillery Regiment of the Seventh Reserve Division. For nearly four long years, he struggled and suffered through the terrors of war. He pastored soldiers and dug their graves—many of them friends. Yet, amid so much darkness and death, Tillich found hope in the peace of Christ, not a religious, otherworldly hope, but the hope that gives one the strength to go on. Romans 8 was especially powerful for him during this time. For Tillich, that passage proclaimed a peace stronger "than the sound of exploding shells, of weeping at open graves, of the sighs of the sick, of the moaning of the dying."[6]

During the war, Tillich took concrete steps toward becoming a professor. He presented two papers to the theology faculty of Halle in July of 1916 and was appointed *Privatdozent*. Although it was not a full professorship, it granted him the right to lecture.

The horrors of war left a mark on Tillich's life. His naive innocence was irrevocably destroyed. Like many Germans during the war, he read Nietzsche in the trenches, which impressed him with a renewed sense of the ecstatic affirmation of life coupled with a brutal critique of bourgeois society and nationalism, which Tillich was beginning to turn his back on and blame for the war. Tillich went into war as a young, traditional, patriotic monarchist and left as a radical critic of capitalism and a staunch proponent of religious socialism.

But his politics were not the only thing significantly affected by the disillusionments of war. He also found that the traditional concepts of God no longer held their weight on the battlefield or as he stood before the graves of his friends and fellow soldiers. The God of bourgeois opti-

---

5. Wilhelm and Marion Pauck, *Paul Tillich: His Life & Thought, vol. 1* (New York: Harper & Row Publishers, 1976), 40.
6. Cited ibid., 49.

mism, who promises that all things will work out for those who believe, was put to death in the war. Tillich became aware, for the first time, of the dire need to replace that outdated concept of God and speak of God in a way that would be existentially relevant to the modern situation of human estrangement.

After the war, Tillich was introduced to psychotherapy, which had a clear effect on him. He wrote later, "I was a barbarian when I returned from the war until a friend introduced me to a few psychoanalytic tricks of living."[7] One of Tillich's most popular books, *The Courage to Be*, offers a powerful exploration of the concepts of anxiety and courage in a way that certainly relates to his own psychological healing. Tillich appreciated psychology, not simply because it was fashionable (though it certainly was that at the time), but most of all, because of the healing power he experienced.

2. Post-war career building

The next stage in Tillich's life involved a growing interest in religious socialism (culminating in his book *The Socialist Decision*, which was later seized and burned by the Nazis), a tendency toward philosophical system building (*The System of the Sciences*, which he began to outline during the war), his first developments of a theology of culture (a significant lifelong preoccupation), and his early successes as a lecturer and professor of both philosophy and theology at various universities.

Tillich's socialism remained fairly idealistic as he actively resisted the materialism of traditional Marxism. Nonetheless, he was a popular exponent of religious socialism in post-war Germany, particularly with his book, *The Religious Situation*, which was one of his first published works to receive a wide audience (though it remains an under-examined text in English). Tillich's larger book on socialism, *The Socialist Decision*, was published too late to make any difference in the fate of the Weimar Republic or the rise of Nazism. However, Tillich later spoke with a sense of pride about how the book was seized and burned by the Nazis, which placed him in the company of great thinkers such as Freud, Einstein, Marx, and Kafka, whose works were also "cleansed" by the fires.

---

7. Cited ibid., 56.

In *The Religious Situation,* Tillich criticized capitalism and endorsed what we might call today "democratic socialism," arguing that socialism, as "the antagonist of the capitalist spirit, in the very act of revolting against the domination of capital, carries the democratic idea through to its logical conclusion."[8] Tillich developed an early concept of *kairos* and argued for an attitude of belief-ful realism, which contrasts believing realism and utopian idealism.[9] His aim with this approach was to navigate between materialism and otherworldly transcendence. An orientation toward the eternal should mean transforming our present situation without claiming to have possessed the eternal in and through our finite attempts at changing things. Thus, religious socialism relies upon the invasion, but not the possession, of the eternal within the finite.

Tillich traces a revolt against capitalism in many spheres, but this revolt is not identical with the movements of communism or utopianism; instead, they were an expression of the *kairos* moment of the eternal breaking into the present situation, which Tillich traces not only in the church but also in culture. More broadly, Tillich's book identified a cultural and religious turning away from the spirit of capitalist society. He promotes an attitude of "belief-ful realism" and the movement of religious socialism, which requires thinking and speaking of this movement "with unconditioned, active responsibility."[10] This book is an important work in Tillich's development, since many of the ideas he later became famous for developing can be found within this early text.

The Socialist Decision is more directly political in nature. It was published in 1933, the same year Hitler came to power. The book reflects on the proletarian situation and argues for a "socialist decision," seeing socialism as a vital resource in confronting the contemporary situation. As early as 1919, Tillich had urged "representatives of Christianity and the church who stand on socialist soil to enter into the socialist movement in order to pave the way for a future union of Christianity and the socialist social order."[11] A key aspect of Tillich's theology of culture is the idea that

---

8. *The Religious Situation,* trans. H. Richard Niebuhr (Cleveland: The World Publishing Company, 1932), 128.
9. Ibid., 174-7.
10. Ibid., 217-8.
11. Cited by John R. Stumme in *The Socialist Decision,* trans. Franklin Sherman (New York: Harper & Row Publishers, 1977), xii n6.

religion is not limited to the religious sphere, but involves all of God's dealings with the world. That means "it is possible that God's activity may be more clearly seen in a profane, even anti-Christian, phenomenon like socialism than in the explicitly religious sphere of the church."[12] At the same time, Tillich argued that socialism cannot be understood without acknowledging its religious dimension, namely, its prophetic and eschatological tendencies.

The book was one of the reasons for Tillich's eventual flight from Germany. According to John Stumme, a Nazi officer from the Ministry of Education, "is reported to have asked Tillich to revoke *The Socialist Decision* in exchange for a prestigious chair in theology at the University of Berlin. Tillich's reply was to laugh in his face."[13] The book became, for Tillich and his friends, a "symbol of courage and resistance."[14] Later in life, Tillich confessed to one of his students—James Luther Adams—that "of all his books, he was most proud of *The Socialist Decision*."[15]

The book is detailed and insightful, and it shows how Tillich's later method of correlation has its roots in his engagement with religious socialism. Socialism, for Tillich, involves the analysis of being, which correlates with the religious ultimate. Both dimensions are vital, which is why Tillich begins the book by describing the socialist decision as a decision *of* and *for* socialism. The decision *of* socialism is a call for socialists to discover the religious dimension of depth in socialism and every political project. The decision *for* socialism is a call for critics of socialism (especially in the church) to make a decision for socialism and against capitalism. In many regards, Tillich's early work on socialism and religion is a precursor to the Christian-Marxist dialogue that took place after World War II.

In 1923, Tillich wrote a systematic outline of scientific disciplines, organized "according to objects and methods," called *The System of the Sciences*. It was Tillich's first large book, published two years before *The Religious Situation*. Tillich ambitiously attempted to organize all fields of knowledge into a system of categorization, according to a conviction that, "In order for an object to be known, it must be assigned its necessary

---

12. Cited ibid., xix.
13. Ibid., xxiv.
14. Ibid.
15. Ibid., xxv.

place within a context."[16] He distinguished between sciences of thought (the ideal sciences), sciences of being (empirical sciences), and sciences of spirit or human sciences (normative sciences). The first category is short and contains subjects like logic and mathematics. The second category is subdivided into three groups, which involve subjects like psychology, biology, technical sciences, and history. The final category is where Tillich places philosophy, art, metaphysics, law, ethics, and theology. He treats theology as "theonomous systematics," indicating how theology establishes the norms of meaning. Theonomy is an important concept for Tillich, which we will explore in chapter one.

This system is a self-consciously "audacious" attempt, but it demonstrates Tillich's passion for creative systematic thought, which can be seen most profoundly in his main work, *Systematic Theology*. Tillich's affinity for system-building is related to his interest in architecture. He saw himself as an architect of ideas.[17] That certainly comes through in his early system as much as his later work.

A final noteworthy contribution during this period was Tillich's first public address, "On the Idea of a Theology of Culture." He presented this lecture on April 16, 1919, at the Kant Society in Berlin. A "theology of culture" is an idea that would continue to pervade much of Tillich's creative work, especially his philosophy of religion and his interest in art, culture, and society. For Tillich, religion is not separate from culture, but represents the "dimension of depth" in *all* of life. His central thesis is that religion is the substance of culture, and culture is the form of religion.

After his first post as a *Privatdozent* in Berlin, Tillich moved between universities until leaving Germany in 1933. He first became associate professor of theology at the University of Marburg from 1924 to 1925, then professor of philosophy and religious studies at Dresden Institute of Technology until 1929, while he was also an adjunct professor of systematic theology at the University of Leipzig from 1927 until 1929, and finally, he was the professor of philosophy at the University of Frankfort until 1933. On April 13, 1933, Tillich was suspended from teaching by

---

16. Paul Tillich, *The System of the Sciences,* trans Paul Wiebe (Lewisburg: Bucknell University Press, 1981), 29.
17. William and Marion Pauck, *Paul Tillich: His Life & Thought* (New York: Harper & Row, Publishers, 1976), 62.

the Nazi government, and he fled to New York, arriving to its shores on November 3, 1933.

While teaching and writing, Tillich's personal life was in turmoil. On January 5, 1920, his beloved sister Johanna died in childbirth. Then, on February 22, 1921, he divorced his first wife, Margaretha (Grethi). She had had an affair with Tillich's close friend, Richard Wegener. Grethi held to a more progressive view of marriage, and she openly mocked Tillich's idea of monogamy. She gave birth to a child from her affair with Wegener. Tillich's own child with Grethi died in infancy. After their divorce, Grethi did not marry Wegener. Tillich felt betrayed by his friend and abandoned by his wife, but he claimed to hold no bitterness toward either of them.

These events drastically shifted Tillich's social relationships, though it is difficult to trace the exact origins of his personal development on this issue. However, it is clear that the once conservative Tillich, who had previously taken vows of celibacy at the Wingolf Society, was now living, post-divorce, like a bohemian with a proclivity for erotic adventures. His apartment became a "pension for struggling artists and students."[18] Tillich's talent for friendship led to many close relationships with women. Several of these turned erotic. Problematically, several such adventures were with students from his classroom, but also with strangers at social events.

Eventually, Tillich met the woman who would become his lifelong partner and wife, Hannah Werner. She was ten years younger than Tillich, but he found her instantly fascinating. Their marriage has been the subject of much speculation (largely in part due to Hannah's book, *From Time to Time*). It was certainly a "tempestuous romance," full of "anguish, passion, and contradiction," but Tillich "forever regarded [Hannah] as the supreme love of his life."[19] They were married on March 22, 1924. They welcomed their first daughter on February 17, 1926.

In July 1932, fighting broke out among the students at the University of Frankfurt. "Storm troopers and Nazi students rioted and beat up left-wing and Jewish students until blood flowed freely."[20] Tillich was enraged by this and took a clear stand against the Nazi students, calling for their

---

18. Ibid., 81.
19. Ibid., 85.
20. Ibid., 127.

expulsion. He made a public speech in defense of the students who were attacked. The event brought Tillich to the attention of the Nazis, and he began to recognize the threat to his life that was posed by Hitler's rise to power. A year later, after many goodbyes and a few close calls with the secret police, he would board a boat with his family and move to America.

3. Life in America and later fame

Tillich's transition to America was a necessary act of self-preservation, but it was exceedingly difficult to leave so many friends behind, especially with such uncertain futures. Tillich did not initially think his move would be permanent. He held out hope for the first few years of life in America that the Nazi regime would fall apart, and he would simply move back and resume his career in Germany. But that illusion gradually and painfully shattered as the war continued.

The first person to welcome Tillich to his new home was Ursula Neibuhr, Reinhold Neibuhr's wife. A visiting professorship had been secured for him by the faculty at Columbia University in the philosophy department for one year and by the Union Theological Seminary faculty as a visiting professor of theology, which later became a more permanent position in 1937. He was known to H. Richard Niebuhr, who had translated *The Religious Situation* into English. But otherwise, Tillich was relatively unknown in America. The professors at Union Theological Seminary voted to donate five percent of their salary to support Tillich during his first year, despite the financial difficulties in America at the time, making it quite a generous gift.

Tillich struggled learning English and initially felt there was little he could learn from America. The pragmatism of American theology and philosophy did not interest the great system-builder and idealist. However, over time, Tillich's thought opened up to American ways of thinking, which eventually affected his style of writing and teaching. Although he never quite accepted the American way completely, his abstract approach benefited from a touch of pragmatism. Tillich observed that American theology was in many ways the opposite of theology in Germany. Theology, the "queen of the sciences," was a mere handmaiden of social ethics in America.[21] But Tillich was able to develop his complex thought in pragmatic ways, without subjecting it to the dominant approach of making theology subservient to ethics. The systematic character of Tillich's theology remained strong, but it was tempered by this new existential practicality that likely contributed to his popularity.

As a professor, Tillich was well-liked by his students, and his lectures were frequently overflowing with attendees. His sermons at the seminary chapel were especially popular, commanding an audience similar in size to that of Billy Graham when he visited to preach. And while the first few years of life in America were difficult, Tillich acclimated well, largely thanks to the academic societies he took part in with his colleagues. He joined the Theological Discussion Group in 1934 and the Philosophy Club at Columbia in the late 1930s or early 1940s. He became full professor of philosophical theology (the first chair of its kind in the country) in 1940, the same year he became a US citizen.

On July 30, 1937, Tillich's father died in Berlin. A year prior, Tillich had published his first autobiographical book, *On the Boundary*, which his father had read and commented on, although his notes to Tillich have been lost. In 1937, a conference was held at Oxford on Tillich's life and work. His theology was becoming more well-known, and the publication of his sermons in 1948, together with a collection of essays under the title *The Protestant Era*, contributed to his growing fame. His growing success culminated in a full professorship, a feature on the cover of Time Magazine, and even a meeting with FDR and his wife, Eleanor Roosevelt, in 1944.

Toward the end of the 1940s, Tillich began working on his *Systematic Theology*, eventually publishing volume one in 1951. The system became an obsession for him. He furiously worked on the volumes, even though it was six years before volume two came out (1957), and another six before volume three completed the system (1963). In between the first and second volumes, Tillich gave lectures at Yale that would later be published as *The Courage to Be*, one of his most popular works. Tillich also presented the famous Gifford Lectures in 1953-4, and he retired from Union in 1955. However, Tillich was quick to take up another position,

---

21. Ibid., 169.

and in 1955, he taught at Harvard University until 1962; he then taught at the University of Chicago until his death in 1965.

Tillich died of a heart attack on October 22, 1965, and his ashes were scattered in New Harmony, Indiana, at the newly dubbed "Paul Tillich Park." Later in life, Tillich became increasingly interested in psychology, a fact that is evident in *The Courage to Be,* but it also reflects his personal experience with psychotherapy after the war. This late interest largely replaced his early preoccupation with politics, even though he never became entirely apolitical. He was disillusioned with the idealism of religious socialism, considering it a far too romantic approach to politics, especially when a realistic one was needed.[22] A trip to Japan opened Tillich up to religious pluralism, and it led him to regret that, if he could start over, his *Systematic Theology* would have been written from the perspective of world religions. He was especially interested in the convergences between Christianity and Buddhist mysticism.

Tillich's influence remains strong today. His overall approach—a philosophical theology that correlates the questions of being with the Christian message—is a powerful apologetic. He analyzed the post-war condition of anxiety with precision and applied the message of justification by grace in an innovative way that has undoubtedly helped many regain the "courage to be." He is a theologian who helped bring the Christian message into the Twentieth Century in a way that can and does speak to the modern person still today. Accordingly, his legacy as one of the greatest theologians of the modern era is secure.

---

22. Ibid., 206.

1. Faith and Doubt

Summary: Genuine faith includes doubt, and honest doubt involves faith. Tillich defines faith as the state of being grasped by an ultimate concern. True faith consists of the uncertainty of doubt because the ultimate is *received* by a finite person bound to the limitations of their finitude, which makes faith a *risk* requiring the courage to accept uncertainty. That is the paradox of faith. Tillich develops from this a definition of orthodoxy and heterodoxy that is more flexible and open to a diversity of opinions. It also leads Tillich to develop a theology of culture based on the conviction that religion is the *substance* of culture, and culture is the *form* of religion.

In Tillich's own words:

> I applied the doctrine of justification to the sphere of human thought. Not only human acts but human thinking as well stand under the divine "No." No one, not even a believer or a church, can boast of possessing truth, just as no one can boast of possessing love. Orthodoxy is intellectual pharisaism. The justification of the doubter corresponds to the justi-

fication of the sinner. Revelation is just as paradoxical as the forgiveness of sins. Neither can become the object of possession.[1]

The affirmation that Jesus is the Christ is an act of faith and consequently of daring courage. It is not an arbitrary leap into darkness but a decision in which elements of immediate participation and therefore certitude are mixed with elements of strangeness and therefore incertitude and doubt. But doubt is not the opposite of faith; it is an element of faith. Therefore, there is no faith without risk. The risk of faith is that it could affirm a wrong symbol of ultimate concern, a symbol which does not really express ultimacy.[2]

Never consider the secular realm Godless just because it does not speak of God. To speak of a realm of divine creation and providence as Godless *is* Godless. It denies God's power over the world. It would force God to confine Godself to religion and church.[3]

SECONDARY QUOTES:

For Paul Tillich, however, the concept of faith refers to something much more comprehensive than a doctrinal affirmation. It identifies a way of life, a centered locus for oneself in the world of competing challenges and values. Simply, faith is a matter of being grasped by an ultimate concern and, in response, focusing completely on one's ultimate concern.[4]

— DONALD W. MUSSER AND JOSEPH L. PRICE

Tillich remains grounded in Luther's central conviction of justification by grace through faith in Jesus the Christ, but re-states this dogma in language appropriate for the modern age, which Tillich believes can no longer understand the traditional terminology tied to the institutional

---

1. Paul Tillich, *On the Boundary* (New York: Charles Scribner's Sons, 1966), 51.
2. Paul Tillich, ST2, 116.
3. Paul Tillich, *The Irrelevance and Relevance of the Christian Message*, ed. Durwood Foster (Eugene, OR: Wipf & Stock, 2007), 62-3.
4. Donald W. Musser and Joseph L. Price, *Tillich* (Nashville: Abingdon Press, 2010), 51.

church. His theological system, with all its complexities and nuances, blossoms from his understanding of justification as divine acceptance in spite of human unacceptability as centered in Luther's theology of the cross.[5]

— Brach S. Jennings

Introduction

Faith and doubt are commonly thought of as oil and water—two incompatible substances. That is because faith is often defined in opposition to doubt. But for Paul Tillich, true faith *includes* doubt, while honest doubt is never without a spark of faith. He argues that the two positions are not opposites but mutually dependent upon one another. It is a unique (and arguably more biblical) concept of faith and doubt that I find exceptionally practical and pastoral.

Why begin at this point in Tillich's theology? Because it not only sets Tillich apart as a truly *modern* theologian—someone who speaks to our present situation—but because it may help clear up some of the misunderstandings circulating about him.

Tillich has many critics, but among the most extreme are those who have suggested that he was actually an atheist in a theologian's clothing. Famously, Leonard F. Wheat wrote in the 1970s, "Tillich's chief claim to fame will be that he fooled a lot of people."[6] Wheat describes this supposed deception: "Tillich is a complete atheist who lost his belief while completing his higher education. Intellectually he despises Christianity.... Still, being the son of a clergyman and having a fondness for religious life... Tillich [will] have his cake and eat it too. He is going to remain with the church for the purpose of undermining Christianity from within."[7] Clearly, this is an uncharitable reading of Tillich's theology—the

---

5. Brach S. Jennings, "The Courage to Be: Paul Tillich's Existentialist Theology of the Cross in Relation to Martin Luther," in *Dialog* 57 (2018), 217.
6. Leonard F. Wheat, *Paul Tillich's Dialectical Humanism* (Baltimore: Johns Hopkins Press, 1970), 276.
7. Ibid., 187. See Alexander J. McKelway's review of this book (archived on Wayback): https://web.archive.org/web/20051109140419/http://theologytoday.ptsem.edu/jul1971/v28-2-bookreview13.htm.

opposite of my aim here—but it has become a common conception of Tillich that persists despite its unsustainability. A close reading of Tillich's work quickly overcomes this misreading.

Wheat's interpretation may be the most extreme example of such a dubious reading of Tillich, but it has a cousin in the less severe critiques that persist, such as those claiming that Tillich's theology is incompatible with the Christian tradition, that is, the "heresy" label. Both stem from a fundamental misunderstanding about how Tillich thinks about faith and doubt—and orthodoxy and heterodoxy—among other subjects we will consider in later chapters.[8] Beginning with faith, doubt, and religion, we will clarify why, for Tillich, there is no such thing as a pure atheism or pure theism, just as there can be no purely sacred or secular culture. Faith is always and necessarily a *paradox* because it involves speaking of conditioned and unconditioned reality, of the finite and infinite. This paradox is a central component of Tillich's thought, and the way he explores it in the context of faith, doubt, and religion will be a helpful entry point before deciphering the nature of the paradox fully.

JUSTIFICATION OF DOUBTERS

It would not be a stretch to suggest that every Protestant, or at least most Western Christians, is familiar with the concept of justification by grace through faith; it is a basic and foundational claim of Reformation theology. The doctrine answers the question of how God saves sinners. One of Tillich's professors, Martin Kähler, called this the "material principle" of Protestantism (while the biblical norm is the "formal principle"). While justification is commonly applied to sin, Tillich goes further and applies it to the situation of doubt (following Kähler). He writes:

> [T]he principle of justification through faith refers not only to the religious-ethical but also to the religious-intellectual life. Not only he who is in sin but also he who is in doubt is justified through faith. The situation

---

8. Another culprit for this misreading is Tillich's concept of God as beyond being, which leads him to suggest that God does not "exist" but is the ground and power of being itself. We will discuss this idea in chapter two.

FAITH AND DOUBT

of doubt, even doubt about God, need not separate us from God. There is faith in every serious doubt...[9]

Justification involves the whole person, not merely our ethical situation as sinners before God, but also our *intellectual* situation as doubters. Thus, justification includes the justification of doubt *through faith*. That would be a baffling admission if we were to accept a definition of faith and doubt as a contradiction, but Tillich's point is to suggest that faith and doubt are *not* opposites.

Doubt does not separate us from God intellectually any more than the presence of sin undoes justification by grace. The human is still a human and thus, they doubt and sin—yet they are justified by grace through faith in spite of their finitude. So, for Tillich, doubt is an inevitable reality of human life. It is what makes us finite. We would not be fully human if it were not for doubt. A better understanding of faith and doubt recognizes that they must coexist simultaneously in the same way that the reformers described the Christian as *Simul Justus et Peccator*—at once justified and sinful. Actually, Tillich goes further and suggests that no true faith is free from doubt, just as no justified person is without sin. The life of faith requires *courage* to go on in spite of the limitations of finitude.

So, what is faith, for Tillich? He thinks the word is one of the most misunderstood and distorted in the Christian vocabulary. It is necessary to redefine faith for today. Tillich's basic definition is this:

Faith is a state of being ultimately concerned.[10]

An "ultimate concern" is whatever concerns a person ultimately, that is, a concern that involves their whole being. It is contrasted with *relative* or *penultimate* concerns. An ultimate concern is an infinite passion for the ultimate, regardless of how we define "the ultimate." For Tillich, the ultimate is only adequately applied to God, but he is intentionally abstract in his language because he is convinced that *all* human beings have *an* ulti-

---

9. Paul Tillich, *The Protestant Era* (Chicago: The University of Chicago Press, 1948), xiv.
10. Paul Tillich, *Dynamics of Faith* (New York: Harper Collins/Perennial Classics, 2001), 1.

mate concern and therefore some kind of faith, whether or not this concern (this faith) is truly ultimate or not.

A few examples of *false* ultimate concerns are money, power, love, or beauty. But none of these objects are truly "ultimate," and therefore, such faiths are faith in an idol. By making a finite concern ultimate, such faith creates a demonic idol out of a finite reality. Those who make money their ultimate concern, for example, do not speak about their idolatry as a type of faith. However, by making money their ultimate concern, they have both idolized it and practiced faith toward it. We can see here how Tillich's definition of faith thus includes a robust critique of idolatry, and it is also noteworthy for not just criticizing idolatry but describing how it develops and how common it is still today. Few people today will lift up altars to Baal, but many, many people worship idols.

But the main point here is to recognize a key aspect of Tillich's claim: *there are no faithless people*. There is not one human being who lacks a concern for something they deem ultimate, something that involves their whole being existentially. Even nihilism is faith in the ultimate meaninglessness of existence, and to uphold that faith is to stake one's existence on the primacy of nonbeing over being. But it is still a form of faith according to Tillich's definition.

Thus, faith as the state of being ultimately concerned *includes* doubt because there is always the risk of holding onto a false ultimate due to the nature of what it is to be a human being. Calvin called the human heart a "factory of idols," and something along those lines is being claimed with Tillich's approach, just in different terms. For Tillich, all human beings are innately drawn to the ultimate, to strive toward transcending their finitude, and that is because the very ground of their being is God, *the* ultimate. But many people will trade an ultimate concern for relative concerns (often unknowingly), making them ultimate, and that is what Tillich calls idolatry. Both faith and doubt are unavoidable, however, and the only question is what someone makes the object of their ultimate concern.

It is important to notice how Tillich's definition of faith consciously avoids thinking about faith as either *intellectual agreement* or *feeling*. Of course, faith *involves* thoughts and feelings, but it is deeper than that. It is more centered, holistic, and embodied; it is a deeply *existential* state of being. Faith describes the state of being of a person who is *grasped by* and then *turned toward* the ultimate. In that situation, both emotion and rationality transcend the limitations of finitude by their being grasped by the ultimate. Faith *is* a finite act and thus limited by finitude, but it is *also* an act "in which the infinite participate beyond the limitations of a finite act."[11] In other words, faith involves both the finite limitations of human doubt and the infinite transcendence of the ultimate, that is, God. *This is the paradox of faith.* And in this, we discover the certainty *and* uncertainty of faith.

Tillich explains, "[F]aith is uncertain in so far as the infinite to which it is related is received by a finite being. This element of uncertainty in faith cannot be removed, it must be accepted. And the element in faith which accepts this is courage."[12] That is what makes faith both certain and uncertain. The infinite, which is the object of our faith, is *received* by a finite being. Finite being is not miraculously transformed into infinite being, and thus, the innate doubt and instability of finitude remain. Therefore, uncertainty in the life of the faithful is inevitable. It cannot be overcome but must be accepted with courage.

We might say that what Tillich is describing is a deeply *incarnational* concept of faith. An incarnational concept of faith involves the paradox of joining together the infinite and finite, the divine and human. Faith, therefore, cannot be purely divine in the sense that it denies our humanity, which includes denying our doubts or our finite limitations as creatures. But neither can faith be a purely human phenomenon without also containing some transcendent element. Tillich is striving to articulate a concept of faith that avoids both errors of an overly divine faith or an overly human one.

The former error is common amongst more conservative or fundamentalist Christians, who define faith in opposition to doubt, and thus, as a sort of "blind" faith in unreasonable truths divinely given from above. The latter error is common amongst more liberal Christians, who define faith purely through what is naturalistic, which sometimes excludes any transcendent element, any ecstatic step beyond the finite. For Tillich, faith is a state of being ultimately concerned, of being grasped by and turned toward the infinite, but it is not a situation that denies the finitude

---

11. Ibid., 18.
12. Ibid., 18-9.

of the person who is grasped, even though they are truly grasped by the infinite.

Therefore, faith is always a *risk* that requires courage. This courage involves *accepting* the uncertainty of faith, an uncertainty that is unavoidable if the ultimate truly *reaches* us in our limitations as finite creatures. But it is also a faith grounded upon the certainty of its object, namely, the ultimate ground and power of our being, which is God. Tillich defines this courage: "Courage as an element of faith is the daring self-affirmation of one's own being in spite of the powers of 'nonbeing' which are the heritage of everything finite."[13] Faith is a risk because it is never without the uncertainty of finitude. If one's ultimate concern turns out to be a false ultimate, then "the meaning of one's life breaks down."[14] Faith involves the core of our being, not just our intellect or emotions. It is an existential concern. We stake our whole being on this concern.

It is important to see that this means rejecting a common definition of faith assumed by many today, even Christians. They define faith as belief in something that is either true or false. If that is what faith means, then "doubt is incompatible with the act of faith."[15] But Tillich thinks, "If faith is understood as being ultimately concerned, doubt is a *necessary element* in it. It is a consequence of the risk of faith."[16] What Tillich means by doubt, then, is not doubt regarding a particular idea or conclusion; it is not belief in a pre-established orthodoxy. Nor is it skepticism like the kind of methodological doubt necessary for all scientific research. Rather, Tillich means "existential doubt." This sort of doubt does not question truth claims; rather, it describes an awareness "of the element of insecurity in every existential truth."[17] Faith accepts this insecurity and "takes it into itself in an act of courage."[18]

It is essential to notice the difference. Faith is not agreement with this or that idea, nor is doubt disagreement. Rather, faith is an existential concern, and thus, doubt is unavoidable because of the insecurities of finitude. Faith is a risk. As such, faith is a courageous act of being grasped by

---

13. Ibid., 19.
14. Ibid., 20.
15. Ibid., 21.
16. Ibid.; emphasis mine.
17. Ibid., 23.
18. Ibid.

an ultimate concern. But faith must accept existential doubt and courageously go on "in spite of" uncertainty. Tillich explains further, "If doubt appears, it should not be considered as the negation of faith, but as an element which was always and will always be present in the act of faith. Existential doubt and faith are poles of the same reality, the state of ultimate concern."[19] In this sense, doubt actually *verifies* true faith. Blind faith, in Tillich's definition, is false faith. True faith includes doubt, and honest doubt involves faith.

This approach to faith is also quite *biblical.* Although Tillich does not argue his point directly from Scripture, there is an interesting passage at the end of Matthew that confirms his approach quite well. Consider how the gospel of Matthew describes the way the disciples reacted to the resurrection: "They worshiped him, *but they doubted*" (28:17, NRSVue; emphasis mine). The disciples are described as both worshiping and doubting. How might such faith and doubt coexist? This version of the text is the most accurate translation. However, the NKJV renders this in a way that seems to mitigate how uncomfortable this passage would be for Christians who define faith and doubt as opposites. The NKJV adds this qualification to the disciples' doubt: "They worshiped Him; but *some* doubted" (emphasis mine). However, the word "some" is not in the original Greek, even if it might be implied.[20] We could argue that the NKJV inserted the word "some" because of the uncomfortable possibility that faith and doubt might coexist, even for the disciples. That concept of faith was imposed into the text. Instead, the text suggests that the disciples both worshiped *and* doubted. Their faith included doubt.

A famous admission from Mark also suggests that the biblical concept of faith is not one that excludes doubt: "I believe; help my unbelief" (Mark 9:24, NRSVue). The mixture of belief and unbelief makes little sense if belief is defined as simple agreement with a fact. Instead, this highlights the paradox of faith, that we are grasped by an ultimate concern in spite of being finite creatures bound to the limitations of doubt.

I would argue that the biblical concept of faith is closer to Tillich's

---

19. Ibid., 25.
20. This passage and its translation disparity was first pointed out to me during a lecture by Dr. Alan Padgett at Luther Seminary.

definition than the fundamentalist one. The Bible does not seem to treat doubt as the opposite of faith. Rather, faith looks like Jacob wrestling with God, Job debating God and man on his heap of ashes, and the disciples doubting even while they worshiped. Faith is an ultimate existential concern, not simply intellectual agreement to a set of unquestionable dogmas. Thus, true faith necessitates doubt, and all serious doubt is a sign of true faith. Faith is not blind acceptance of a fact. Faith is *courage* in the face of insecurity.

Tillich's approach to faith is liberating: "Many Christians, as well as members of other religious groups, feel anxiety, guilt and despair about what they call 'loss of faith.' But serious doubt is confirmation of faith. It indicates the seriousness of the concern, its unconditional character."[21] I can personally attest to this.

I vividly remember the anxiety I felt as a young believer over the possibility of losing my faith. It was a perpetual anxiety that made faith seem like a fragile, delicate thing that I must protect at all costs. Even today, the language we still use about those who leave Christianity is to say they "lost their faith." Tillich's concept of faith has the potential to liberate us from this anxiety and recognize that embracing uncertainty does not mean losing faith. Instead, faith necessarily includes the uncertainty of finitude. There is room for us to breathe easily and accept this uncertainty with courage, rather than suppressing it with anxiety. To some extent, fundamentalism is simply the denial of uncertainty and the attempt to find certainty above the realities of finitude (either in a book or dogma). But it is an attempt that's doomed to fail, as so many post-fundamentalist and exvangelical Christians can attest to.

Faith Communities

It is necessary to add here that Tillich's concept of faith is not individualistic. Instead, faith involves gathering a community united by a shared ultimate concern. This point leads us to consider Tillich's helpful redefinition of orthodoxy and heterodoxy. A faith community that unites over *agreement* often misuses the term "heresy" to exclude uncertainty, thus denying the very nature of faith in the process by mistaking it with intellectual

---

21. Ibid.

agreement. Heretics, by definition, are excommunicated. But what would it look like to think about the church according to Tillich's concept of faith as a state of being grasped by an ultimate concern?

For Tillich, a better concept of heresy defines it as turning away from "the true to a false, ultimate concern."[22] Only this turning away qualifies for exclusion from the faith community. Heresy, in the sense of agreement, is an inadequate concept. And in fact, Tillich might argue that those who take faith's ultimate concern and turn it into the belief in a doctrine, or an infallible book or pope, or some other dogmatic claim— *these* are the people who turn away from the genuine ultimate concern by making these finite concerns ultimate. Faith is not intellectual agreement, and therefore, heresy is not a game of deciding whose "in" and "out" based on whether or not they agree with a fixed dogma. Instead, a faith community is united by its ultimate concern. And because faith is never certain, there is freedom for a variety of interpretations of the symbols of faith (doctrine), without a loss of community.

In this framework, diversity and difference over theological issues would be *encouraged* rather than being treated as a threat to unity. If orthodoxy means conformity, then orthodoxy itself is a threat to authentic faith because conformity removes every element of risk and courage, which Tillich thinks are essential to genuine faith. He writes, "They have transformed faith into a behavior pattern which does not admit alternatives, and which loses its character of ultimacy even if the fulfillment of the religious duties is done with ultimate concern."[23]

Theology is a finite concern, which, when it is treated as ultimate, becomes an idol. Orthodoxy easily becomes an idol when it is treated with more ultimacy than *the* ultimate to which it bears witness. Theology, in other words, is a finite discipline and thus prone to uncertainty. There is no ultimate theology. The church's theology must not be identified with God. That seems like a basic point, but it is vital to protect theology from idolatry. Treating theological agreement as the highest good is a step toward idolizing *our* theology over the transcendent God, who is beyond even our best thoughts about God. Augustine was right: *Si comprehendis, non est Deus*—if you comprehend it, it is not God. To mistake *our human*

---

22. Ibid., 29.
23. Ibid., 31.

attempts at comprehending God—that is, our orthodox theology—with the ultimate is to practice idolatry.

These points indicate how Tillich's concept of faith is not only personally helpful but can guide conversations about the community of faith for a situation in which "heresy hunters" are quick to exclude everyone who disagrees with their very narrow view of orthodoxy. If faith is agreement, then we are saved by correct doctrine—but that is a denial of the message of divine grace.

Faith always involves risk because of the unavoidable insecurity of finitude. Faith communities will often try to immunize themselves from this risk by claiming an infallible authority as their foundation. That is accomplished, in Catholicism, by the infallible pope, or, in fundamentalism, by the infallible Bible. For Tillich, such efforts make a penultimate and conditional reality (a person or book) into a false ultimate. But no conditional reality can be elevated to the status of ultimacy. Only *the* ultimate, that is, God, who is the ground and power of being, is a true ultimate worthy of faith; every other pseudo-ultimate is an idol. But due to the insecurities inherent to faith, faith communities attempt to elevate a conditional object above the limitations of finitude, and therefore, remove any risk in faith by grounding it upon an infallible authority. Accordingly, this definition of faith means submission to this or that authority, while doubt is excluded as a threat.

That is sometimes why doubt is feared with such anxiety in the church: it represents a threat to the authority of an idol raised to the status of an ultimate and thus falsely endowed with infallible qualities. But no finite reality can transcend the insecurities of finitude. And that is true whether we are talking about a pope or the Bible, or any other finite reality that is elevated to ultimacy, such as a particular doctrine. No finite authority can adequately avoid the insecurities inherent to finitude, despite all our best efforts to the contrary. The ultimate is not afraid of our doubt and insecurity. God is the one who gives us the courage to face the risks of faith, not suppress those risks by elevating external mediums to ultimacy.

Faith is and always will be a *paradox* because faith is incarnational (i.e., embodied in finitude). Only the unconditional is certain. But the unconditional is conveyed to us in and through the conditional, and that is why faith *always* involves insecurity and doubt. We do not *possess* the unconditional; the opposite is true: we are grasped by the ultimate. But we remain finite in the process. Thus, any attempt at removing the human element of faith results in a Docetic (divine without human) appeal to infallible sources, such as the Bible or a pope.

Tillich suggests, in contrast, what he calls the "Protestant principle:"

> How can a faith which has doubt as an element within itself be united with creedal statements of the community of faith? The answer can only be that creedal expressions of the ultimate concern of the community must include their own criticisms. It must become obvious in all of them —be they liturgical, doctrinal or ethical expressions of the faith of the community—that they are not ultimate. Rather, their function is to point to the ultimate which is beyond all of them.[24]

The claims of every faith community *point* to the ultimate, but those claims must not be confused with the ultimate. The Protestant principle thus involves an inbuilt critique of *every* finite expression of faith for the sake of the ultimate to which it points. It is idolatrous to take a conditioned, finite object, deny its limitations, and elevate it to the status of ultimacy. Tillich connects the Protestant principle to a "theology of the cross" because every faith community stands under the judgment of the ultimate over the expressions of finite religion.[25] A faith that does not accept its insecurity and tries to ground itself on a false ultimate is idolatrous. It is not faith in an ultimate concern but a faith that makes a conditioned concern into an ultimate one.

Religion and Theonomy

This understanding of faith and doubt leads us to consider how Tillich thinks about religion. It is clear that whatever religion is, it is not simply agreement or disagreement over certain dogmas. Rather, for Tillich, religion is profoundly existential. He summarizes this point well:

---

24. Ibid., 33.
25. Ibid.

> Religion is being ultimately concerned about that which is and should be our ultimate concern. This means faith is the state of being grasped by an ultimate concern, and God is the name for the content of the concern. Such a concept of religion has little in common with the description of religion as the belief in the existence of a highest being called God, and the theoretical and practical consequences of such a belief. Instead, we are pointing to an existential, not theoretical, understanding of religion.[26]

Tillich challenges the common idea that religion is purely about belief in a theoretical being called "God," which reduces religion to purely conceptual or abstract realms. Instead, he talks about religion as an existential concern with the ultimate ground of being. He is not saying that God is false, but that religion is not simply about the abstract belief in God. In that regard, Tillich's description is arguably closer to the biblical concept of religion because faith in Jesus Christ or Jehovah was never an abstract belief in a concept or feeling, but a personal, communal, and existential concern with the ultimate.

The Israelites did not merely "believe" in *a* God. They courageously risked their very existence on *this* God—YHWH—as their liberator from Egyptian captivity, their sustainer in the wilderness, and their conqueror against foreign gods. The Israelites staked their existence on the ultimacy of their God. Likewise, the disciples and the first Christians risked their lives because of their ultimate concern that Jesus is the Christ, which led to radical self-sacrifice and martyrdom.

Included with this definition of religion is Tillich's unique approach to culture. He challenges the so-called sacred and secular divide:

> If religion is the state of being grasped by an ultimate concern, this state cannot be restricted to a special realm. The unconditional character of this concern implies that it refers to every moment of our life, to every space and every realm. The universe is God's sanctuary. Every work day is a day of the Lord, every supper a Lord's supper, every work the fulfillment of a divine task, every joy a joy in God. In all preliminary concerns, ulti-

---

26. Paul Tillich, *Theology of Culture* (Oxford: Oxford University Press, 1959), 40.

mate concern is present, consecrating them. Essentially the religious and the secular are not separate realms. Rather they are within each other.[27]

If religion means simply a belief in something, then the sacred-secular divide makes sense because the sacred believes, while the secular does not. But Tillich breaks down that divide. No aspect of life is irrelevant to one's ultimate concern, or else it would not be truly ultimate. And no person, no matter how secular, is without an ultimate concern. That is a consequence of Tillich's move to understand both faith and religion existentially, rather than purely intellectually or spiritually.

It is important to note here that both the intellect and spirit take part in our ultimate concern—Tillich is not excluding either. Rather, he is aiming for a more robust concept of religion beyond either the purely spiritual or intellectual definitions. For example, an ultimate concern is present whenever a scientist investigates the nature of the universe, which means faith need not contradict the conclusions of science. Rather, the preliminary concerns of a scientist about their theories is deeply related to being grasped by an ultimate concern, namely, of a God who is the ground and power of being. The work that a scientist does in uncovering the mysteries of the natural order is *holy work* and the claim that faith and science exist at war with one another operates with faulty definitions.

Religion that is defined as belief in God not only relies on a faulty concept of faith, but it also misunderstands the nature of God. Tillich defines religion apart from the question of God's existence because he finds that the question misunderstands the radical distinction between God and the world. This has led to the mistaken claim that Tillich is an atheist who merely retains the shape of religion without the content, but that fails not only in understanding how Tillich defines faith but also his crucial move to understand God as the God who is necessarily *beyond* existence.

Tillich writes, "If you start with the question whether God does or does not exist, you can never reach Him; and if you assert that He does exist, you can reach Him even less than if you assert that He does not exist. A God about whose existence or non-existence you can argue is a

---

27. Ibid., 41.

thing beside others within the universe of existing things."[28] God is not a thing among other created things that we might prove like an apple or a scientific theory. Instead, God, as creator, is beyond being and thus non-objectifiable. Tillich strives to take God *seriously as God.* That is why he defines religion apart from the existence or non-existence of God—because, as Dietrich Bonhoeffer explains, "A god who could be proved by us would be an idol."[29] Religion as the state of being grasped by an ultimate concern is not about proving God; rather, it is an existential concern with the unconditional and ultimate. Therefore, "ultimate concern is manifest in all creative functions of the human spirit."[30]

God must be presupposed in the question of God, or else theology risks turning God into an object. Accordingly, Tillich's definition of religion presupposes God as the basis of our questions, not as the object arrived at through our questioning. Because God is the power and ground of being (a concept we will explore more in the next chapter), the question of God's existence is not the first question in religion. If God is truly God, then God must transcend the status of being merely a thing among other created things, which calls the provability of God into question.

This point connects with the uncertainty of faith. It is impossible, as finite creatures, to avoid uncertainty. As much as fundamentalism deludes itself into thinking it might find unquestionable certainty with a set of dogmas, or in the infallibility of either a pope or a book. None of these can remove the uncertainty of finitude.

With the division of a sacred and secular realm removed, Tillich then proposes a *theology of culture* that more adequately reflects the presence of ultimate concern in all areas of life. He argues that religion is the "substance" of culture, while culture is "a form of expression" of religion.[31] Religion is directed toward the "unconditional meaning," while culture is directed toward "conditional forms."[32] That leads Tillich to an important concept, which he calls "theonomy." He describes it as "the unity of reli-

---

28. Paul Tillich, *Theology of Culture* (Oxford: Oxford University press, 1959), 5.
29. Dietrich Bonhoeffer, *Ecumenical, Academic, and Pastoral Work: 1931-1932* (Minneapolis, MN: Fortress Press, 2012), 260.
30. Paul Tillich, *Theology of Culture* (Oxford: Oxford University Press, 1959), 8.
31. Paul Tillich, *What is Religion?* (New York: Harper & Row Publishers, 1973), 73.
32. Ibid., 72.

gion and culture... a unity of unconditioned meaning-import and of conditioned meaning-form..."[33]

In contrast with theonomy, Tillich describes "autonomy" as culture without ultimacy. What remains, then, is form without substance: "Autonomy therefore is always at the same time obedience to and revolt against the Unconditional. It is obedience insofar as it subjects itself to the unconditioned demand for meaning; it is revolt insofar as it denies the unconditioned meaning itself."[34] Thus, autonomous culture asks the question of meaning but rejects the unconditional substance that alone can provide an answer. In contrast, a third concept is raised by Tillich, that of "heteronomy." Whereas autonomy is culture without religious substance, heteronomy is religion without cultural form. Thus, autonomy revolts against the unconditional, whereas heteronomy denies the conditional.

In contrast, theonomy is the unity of both religion and culture, and it is symbolized in Christian thought with the kingdom of God. Thus, it is an eschatological concept, but not in the sense that it has no relevance to the here and now. Instead, theonomy is the basis for a theology of culture. So, for example, Tillich can analyze the religious substance of cultural forms such as art and architecture. He analyzes Picasso's famous Guernica painting as a "great Protestant painting" that powerfully puts before us the "question of man in a world of guilt, anxiety, and despair."[35] That point builds upon the conviction that no one can escape religion even if they reject it, "for religion is the state of being ultimately concerned. And in every [artistic] style the ultimate concern of a human group or period is manifest."[36]

The benefit of Tillich's definition of religion is that it recognizes the religious depth of culture and engages with that depth in interesting ways. Religion, then, is "at home everywhere" because it is "the aspect of depth in the totality of the human spirit."[37] The reason why religion has been compartmentalized into a separate space called the "sacred" is that

---

33. Ibid., 74. It is important to note that theonomy is *not* theocracy. A theocracy is what Tillich calls heteronomy, which is the dominance of the religious over and against the cultural. Theonomy is a synthesis and transcendence of both heteronomy and autonomy.
34. Ibid., 75.
35. Paul Tillich, *Theology of Culture* (Oxford: Oxford University Press, 1959), 68-9.
36. Ibid., 70.
37. Ibid., 7.

humankind is alienated from its spiritual life. Therefore, Tillich argues that the divide between sacred and secular is a result of the fall and a sign of sin.

Another important aspect of Tillich's theology of culture is that he envisions it as a new kind of ethics. That is because the aims of theological ethics "can only be realized by means of a theology of culture applying not only to ethics but to all the functions of culture."[38] It is not enough to discuss ethics as a special function of theology; instead, a theology of culture is more expansive in analyzing the form of the religious substance in cultural expressions.

For Tillich, there are three tasks set before a theology of culture: "1. General religious analysis of culture. 2. Religious typography and philosophy of cultural history. 3. Concrete religious systematization of culture."[39] A theology of culture thus seeks to uncover the religious meaning of society, despite its claims of secularization. Religion and culture *are* united even while attempts at autonomy and heteronomy persist. That is so because no cultural expression lacks religious depth—consciously or unconsciously—and no religious substance lacks cultural expression (because even an infinite concern must be expressed with finite language and thus through culture).

Accordingly, Tillich does not think a purely autonomous or heteronomous situation exists, even if movements toward either polarity persist. However, Tillich rejects the tendency to construct two separate ethics, either one for the sacred or another for the secular. Ethical reflection must be based upon the unity of religion and culture, not their disunity. William Schweiker helpfully explains, "Theology of culture links the theoretical and the practical, the scientific and the moral, by articulating the meaning-giving power of human activities."[40] A theology of culture is thus a unifying concept for thinking about how to live and speak about one's ultimate concern in society, and that includes ethical reflection. In this sense, Tillich's concept of a theology of culture is a remarkable expression of the unity of human life, despite its disunity, in

---

38. Paul Tillich, *What is Religion?* (New York: Harper & Row Publishers, 1973), 160.
39. Ibid., 165; original italics removed.
40. William Schweiker, "Theology of Culture and its future" in *The Cambridge Companion to Paul Tillich,* ed. Russel Re Manning (Cambridge: Cambridge University Press, 2009), 139.

the eschatological expectation of a theonomous culture, which is symbolized in Christian theology with the kingdom of God.

Conclusion

This chapter has considered several points related to Tillich's definition of faith and doubt, religion, and theonomy. These concepts are a helpful entry to Tillich's complex theology because they indicate how he thinks. But as we proceed further into Tillich's thought, they will come up again. That is something I have often found true about Tillich: his work is deeply interconnected. So if these concepts are not yet clear, stay patient because they might become clearer in other contexts.

I also wanted to start with these ideas because I think they are especially practical ones for today's world. I find myself referring to Tillich's concept of faith quite regularly in conversations with friends and family. His approach is liberating but also challenging. It liberates us from the compartmentalizing tendency of faith and opens us up to recognizing the holy in the profane. But it is challenging because it means we must courageously face the uncertainties of life in a finite world; we cannot hide away in the false certainties of a separate sacred space that, for Tillich, simply does not exist.

Sermon: The Divine Name

One of the foundational ideas guiding Tillich's concept of faith and doubt is his doctrine of God. In a sermon on the name of God, he explores this connection. His text is Exodus 20:7, "You shall not take the name of the Lord your God in vain…" There is power in a name, especially in God's name. "A name is never an empty sound; it is a bearer of power; it gives Spiritual Presence to the unseen. This is the reason the divine name can be taken in vain…"[1] There is a great danger both in religion and "anti-religion" to misuse God's name. But there is also an embarrassment that sometimes arises with the name of God, which Tillich categorizes into three forms: the embarrassment of tact, doubt, and awe.

"I hope for the day when everyone can speak again of God without embarrassment." This quote is sometimes attributed to Tillich, but it is attributed *mistakenly*. It is the very opposite of what he wants to argue. He cites this quote in his sermon and attributes it to "an intellectual leader," but, ironically, it has become a phrase attributed to Tillich, who directly argues against the idea that there will ever be a day when we can speak the name of God without embarrassment. Because if that were the case, then we would, in some way, lay claim to God and possess God's name like a tool or object. For Tillich, God is non-objectifiable. God

---

1. Paul Tillich, *The Eternal Now* (New York: Charles Scribner's Sons, 1963), 93.

must remain beyond our grasp. Tillich asks, "Is an unembarrassed use of the divine name desirable? Is unembarrassed religion desirable? Certainly not! For the Presence of the divine in the name demands a shy and trembling heart."[2] The domestication of God is a severe danger, and it is one that violates the second commandment to keep the name of God holy.

There is something theologically liberating in this: *It is embarrassing to speak of God.* The theologian's role is not to mitigate this embarrassment. The opposite is true: It is the theologian who must perpetually remind us that to speak of God is a radical, messy, embarrassing, yet profoundly courageous and deeply human act. It is not for the faint of heart. The phenomenon of the holy, which is a central component of Tillich's thought, is not our's to domesticate. It is our job to let the living God remain living. A domestic God—a safe God—is an idol; we theologians must be concerned with the undomesticated, living God. Only this God satisfies the criteria for an infinite passion and ultimate concern. Letting God be God means embracing the embarrassment of daring to speak of such a God whom we cannot control.

There is an inherent risk in theology; it requires courage because of the severity of speaking God's name, of daring to describe or give attributes to God. Tillich writes, "The sublime embarrassment about [God's] real Presence in and through His name should never leave us."[3] This embarrassment is unavoidable; the alternative of taking God's name in vain is far worse than whatever embarrassment arises from speaking of the living God. It is a radical thing to speak of God, an act of courage that should not be taken lightly. We tactfully navigate between silence and this courageous speaking because of the embarrassment rooted in deep awe before a holy God.

Beyond these two types of embarrassment—tact and awe—Tillich also considers the "more basic" cause for embarrassment: doubt. Here, too, embarrassment is necessary. For Tillich, "[D]oubt is universally human..."[4] It is unavoidable that human beings daring to speak of God would be full of doubt. Thus, doubt is necessary; it is not the result of faithlessness but quite the opposite: true faith includes doubt because it

---

2. Ibid., 94.
3. Ibid., 95.
4. Ibid., 96.

takes seriously the One it has faith in. Tillich explains that "God would not be God if we could possess Him like any object of our familiar world, and verify His reality like any other reality under inquiry."[5] This point relates to the dubious practice of "proving" the existence of God. But God is not like an atomic element or an undiscovered island. We cannot verify or grasp the evidence of the divine reality because of the categorical difference between God and nature. God is not *a* being among others but the ground and power of being.

Tillich continues:

> Unless doubt is conquered, there is no faith. Faith must overcome something; it must leap over the ordinary processes that provide evidence, because its object lies above the whole realm where scientific verification is possible. Faith is the courage that conquers doubt, not by removing it, but by taking it as an element into itself. I am convinced that the element of doubt, conquered in faith, is never completely lacking in any serious affirmation of God. It is not always on the surface; but it always gnaws at the depth of our being.[6]

Tillich thinks we often repress doubt with fanatical, unquestioning affirmations, but doubt cannot be eliminated from faith. To doubt is human. Though conquered, doubt is a part of faith because of the difference between God and humanity. There is no ultimate certainty in either affirming or denying the existence of God. As human beings, we cannot avoid this doubt. "Doubt, and not certitude, is our human situation, whether we affirm or deny God. And perhaps the difference between them is not so great as one usually thinks."[7] The opposite of faith is not doubt but indifference. Doubt means one takes seriously the object of faith. Indifference is far more dangerous in its implications.

Thus, for Tillich, doubt is another cause of our sublime embarrassment, which is "an expression of conscious or unconscious honesty."[8] Ultimately, however, behind this embarrassment "lies something more

---

5. Ibid.
6. Ibid., 96-7.
7. Ibid., 97.
8. Ibid., 98.

fundamental, the silence of awe, that seems to prohibit the speaking of God altogether."[9] That does not mean resigning ourselves to silence and indifference. "Must we spread silence around what concerns us more than anything else—the meaning of our existence? The answer is—no! For God Himself has given mankind names for Himself...."[10] God names Godself, and therefore, we cannot fall into total silence. The true power of silence is when someone else is speaking. In this sense, the silence of awe is itself a kind of speaking, but one that deeply respects the otherness of God. Tillich beautifully describes the church along these lines, "The church is the place where the mystery of the holy should be experienced with awe and sacred embarrassment."[11]

Tillich's sermon helpfully articulates the reasons why faith and doubt are not opposites, but that true faith includes doubt, and no doubt is completely free of faith. This dynamic exists because of the nature of human beings in our finitude, but also because of the otherness of God. Yet God names Godself in an act of grace toward us, and we are entrusted with the command to keep that name holy. Any theology that speaks of God as if God were an object we might control or use is an example of misusing the name of God and taking it in vain. There are countless examples of taking God's name in vain: evoking God's name to endorse violent wars against foreigners or strangers, to promote militarism and imperialism, not to mention the misuse of God's name to enforce Christofascist policies. We might even argue that any act of injustice against human beings or the created order is a misuse of the name of God because God is the ground and power of being itself.

However, in the context of this chapter, it is vital to see how Tillich's approach to faith and doubt is profound in its respect for the divine nature. The goal of his theology is *not* to make it less embarrassing to speak of God in a modern context. Instead, he affirms the unavoidable fact that it is sublimely embarrassing to speak the name of God, but that we must go on speaking of God with courage. In that context, he aims to speak of God in a way that is *meaningful* for the modern person. And any attempt at making theology less embarrassing goes against that aim.

---

9. Ibid., 99.
10. Ibid.
11. Ibid.

2. God and Being

Summary: Tillich's concept of symbolic God-talk and doctrine of God coincide in the conviction that God is *holy* yet *related*—that is, God is not an object we might control, but God is closer to us than we are to ourselves. God is the ground and power of being-itself, while God is also beyond essence and existence. The traditional attributes of God are reassessed in this framework, as God is the power of being that overcomes the threats of nonbeing in the categories of power, space, time, and knowledge. And ultimately, God is the love that reunites the estranged, and God is just.

In Tillich's own words:

> A religious symbol uses the material of ordinary experience in speaking of God, but in such a way that the ordinary meaning of the material used is both affirmed and denied. Every religious symbol negates itself in its literal meaning, but it affirms itself in its self-transcending meaning. It is not a sign pointing to something with which it has no inner relationship.

It represents the power and meaning of what is symbolized through participation. The symbol participates in the reality which is symbolized.[1]

God is the basic and universal symbol for what concerns us ultimately.[2]

But the real situation with which we are faced is the loss of the power of religious symbols in general. We can no longer speak of God easily to anybody because he will immediately question, 'Does he exist?' Now the very asking of the question signifies that the symbols of God have become meaningless. For God, in the question, has become one of innumerable objects in time and space which may or may not exist. And this is not the meaning of God at all.[3]

Secondary quotes:

God is not a hypothesis, which could be verified or falsified, but God is the thesis that is always already presupposed by every claim to truth and every statement about being or about the unconditional.[4]

— Martin Leiner

Because all that exists is grounded in and sustained by God, all initiative for what is commonly called the divine-human encounter actually originates in God. On their own, then, persons cannot arrive at knowledge of God or even at a symbolic apprehension of God. The awareness of God is innate in human experience because by existing, a person participates in being, which is the power of God.[5]

— Donald W. Musser and Joseph L. Price

---

1. Paul Tillich, ST2, 9.
2. Paul Tillich, *Love, Power, and Justice* (Oxford: Oxford University Press, 1954), 109.
3. Paul Tillich, *Ultimate Concern*, ed. D. Mackenzie Brown (New York: Harper & Row, 1965), 88.
4. Martin Leiner, "Tillich on God" in *The Cambridge Companion to Paul Tillich*, ed. Russel Re Manning (Cambridge: Cambridge University Press, 2009), 44.
5. Donald W. Musser and Joseph L. Price, *Tillich* (Nashville: Abingdon Press, 2010), 21.

God and Being

> Tillich presumes that God meets us where we are.[6]
>
> — Daniel J. Peterson

Introduction

This chapter considers Tillich's doctrine of God and the conviction that only symbolic language is appropriate when speaking of God. Symbols are necessary, for Tillich, to preserve the ultimacy of faith's ultimate concern, or, in other words, to protect the otherness of God. But it is also necessary to rightly speak about God's *relatedness*, that God is closer to us than we are to ourselves, which Tillich creatively implements through his definition of God as the ground and power of being, or being-itself. Thus, the two concerns are closely related: to speak of God as truly ultimate requires symbolic language.

Tillich's doctrine of God is unique but not altogether unprecedented. He talks about God as the ground and power of being, who is the answer to the question of finite being. We will first consider the nature of symbols and God as being-itself before looking at four classic attributes of God: omnipotence, eternity, omnipresence, and omniscience. Finally, we conclude with the foundational reality that God is love and just.

It is essential to underline that, for Tillich, God is not an abstract, speculative being. Instead, God is existentially related to our situation as creatures living under the conditions of finitude, which involves the continual threat of nonbeing (of death). God, as the ground and power of being, is the God of love who triumphs over nonbeing. Tillich's doctrine of God, then, is profoundly soteriological (that is, related to salvation). God is chiefly the one who saves and overcomes, and that is why God is the answer to the question implied in being.

With this chapter, we are also stepping into Tillich's *Systematic Theology*. The system contains five parts: reason and revelation, being and God, existence and Christ, life and the spirit, and history and the kingdom of God. We will return to the first section on reason and revelation when

---

6. Daniel J. Peterson, *Tillich: A Brief Overview of the Life and Writings of Paul Tillich* (Minneapolis: Lutheran University Press, 2013), 83.

considering Tillich's method, but this chapter focuses on section two on "being and God." The remaining chapters follow Tillich's outline in order.

Symbolic God-talk

What does Tillich mean by a symbol? He often explains this by contrasting *symbols* with *signs*. Both a sign and a symbol point beyond themselves. However, only a symbol *participates* in what it indicates, while a sign only points. For example, a red stop sign points to a traffic law that drivers must follow, but it does not participate in the act of stopping a car or the legal system itself. It merely points. Therefore, signs can be replaced without a fundamental change in the law.

A symbol, however, points beyond itself while also participating in what it indicates. Tillich often used the example of a nation's flag to explain the difference; the American flag participates in the "power and dignity of the nation for which it stands."[7] The famous "stars and stripes" cannot be replaced as easily as a stop sign. That is because the American flag participates in the power and meaning of what it symbolizes; it is not merely a neutral, easily exchangeable pointer. These are Tillich's first two points about symbols.

His third point about symbolic language is that it "opens up levels of reality which otherwise are closed for us."[8] Tillich's example for this is art and poetry, which reveal something about life and the world that cannot be expressed scientifically or with ordinary speech. Symbols open up a reality previously closed to us by the conceptual tools available.

But the symbol cuts both ways. Tillich's fourth point is that a symbol not only opens up something about the reality it points to, but also something in ourselves. A poem grasps at an indescribable reality, but it also reveals something about our souls as we read it. Thus, symbols have this twofold character. Great art and symbols are those that open up new levels of reality and ourselves at once. Likewise, a religious symbol opens up new ways of speaking about God, but it may also open new ways of relating to the ultimate. Tillich calls this the "main function of a symbol"

---

7. Paul Tillich, *Dynamics of Faith* (New York: Harper Collins, 1957), p. 48.
8. Ibid.

because it is only in this way that an ultimate concern might be understood.⁹

Tillich's fifth claim is that symbols cannot be invented. "They grow out of the individual or collective unconscious and cannot function without being accepted by the unconscious dimension of our being."¹⁰ What Tillich means here is that symbols have a social function. That leads to a sixth point: symbols die only when the social function from which they arise changes, that is, the situation. "They die," Tillich writes, "because they can no longer produce response in the group where they originally found expression."¹¹

These six points articulate the characteristics of all symbolic language, particularly religious symbols. A key symbol for religion is "God." By calling God a symbol, we must keep in mind these six points. What Tillich is *not* suggesting is that God is merely a *myth* without any reality behind it or a *sign* that fails to truly participate in what it indicates. When people first read Tillich's work, his frequent use of the word "symbol" can lead to the impression that he uses symbols in the same way as others might use the terms myths or signs. But Tillich is not saying that these symbols are myths. Instead, Tillich uses the term "symbol" in a specific way, and it is rooted in his theological commitment to God's otherness *and* relatedness, which is why I have decided to introduce his concept of symbols in connection with his doctrine of God.

So, as a symbol, the word "God" points beyond itself while also participating in what it indicates. That is because "no finite reality can express it [ultimacy] directly and properly."¹² In the previous chapter, we discussed how finite concerns that become ultimate are idols; faith, however, is the state of being grasped by an *ultimate* concern. That leads to the paradox of faith: it involves being grasped by an infinite concern yet being bound to finite reality. Thus, doubt and risk are unavoidable because of the limitations of finitude.

Similarly, symbols are a way to express the state of being grasped by an infinite concern within the limitations of finitude, to indicate what is meant by "the ultimate." Tillich is convinced we can only speak of this

---

9. Paul Tillich, *The Ground of Being*, ed. Robert M. Price (Mindvendor, 2015), 301.
10. Paul Tillich, *Dynamics of Faith* (New York: Harper Collins, 1957), 49.
11. Ibid., 50.
12. Ibid., 51.

paradox through symbolic language. Finite God-talk would be idolatry if it tried to express *directly* the reality of God without qualifying theology as symbolic language.

Most of us already do this without realizing it. When I talk about God, I am conscious that the English word "God" is not inherent to the reality indicated by it. The word God is not literal, in other words. However, I am also aware that this word participates in the reality it indicates because it has a social function as a symbol. That means the reality indicated by the word God is *real,* but because God is infinite, finite speech cannot directly express God. The sacred tetragram YHWH functions similarly. It was (and still is) revered as an unspeakable stand-in for the name of God, yet the fact that this tetragram was given to human beings at all reveals God's vulnerable desire to be known by God's people. God wills to be named (and thus, God becomes vulnerable enough to allow humanity to call upon God) while also demanding that this name be kept holy. This paradox comes close to what Tillich is expressing with his concept of symbolic language.

If God were an object like an apple, symbolic language wouldn't be necessary. But because God is wholly other yet related, symbols are essential. Tillich explains, "Religiously speaking, God transcends his own name."[13] If God did not transcend the word "God," then God would be an idol. But, on the other hand, if the word "God" completely failed to participate in the reality it indicates, then it would just be a word without any reality behind it. "God" would simply be a projection of ourselves, as Feuerbach suggested. Thus, in contrast to Feuerbach, symbolic language is necessary to protect both the Godness of God and the humanity of all human speech about God. God transcends God's own name, yet God also wills to be known and thus spoken about by human beings.

The dual error Tillich avoids might be expressed like this: If the symbol "God" becomes *literal,* then it is idolatrous; if it becomes merely a sign, then it ceases to be religious in the sense that it loses its place as a truly *ultimate* concern—it is just another human word without transcendent meaning.

What this means in practice is that all human speech about God contains a ready-made, built-in critique, which Tillich called the Protes-

---

13. Ibid.

tant principle. All religious language stands under the judgement of ultimacy by its nature as human language within the conditions of finitude. When symbols are taken literally, they lose their ultimacy. That is because God must transcend even our naming of God.

In the previous chapter, I mentioned how the Protestant principle relates to Tillich's *theologia crucis,* that is, his "theology of the cross." Tillich's concept of symbols is also profoundly related to the crucified Christ because every symbol necessarily negates its literal meaning while affirming what it points to beyond itself. That dual negating and transcending function relates to Jesus as the Christ who dies to transcend the finitude of his existence and become universal. Tillich explains that the symbol "messiah" or "Christ" is paradoxical in the sense that it is affirmed through self-transcendence. "He who is Christ," Tillich writes, "has to die for his acceptance of the title 'Christ'" (ST2, 97). Elsewhere, Tillich explains:

> If Christianity claims to have a truth superior to any other truth in its symbolism, then it is the symbol of the cross in which this is expressed, the cross of the Christ. He who himself embodies the fullness of the divine's presence sacrifices himself in order not to become an idol, another god beside God, a god into whom the disciples wanted to make him.[14]

Whenever a religious symbol is ultimate *in itself,* it becomes an idol. "All idolatry is nothing else than the absolutizing of symbols of the Holy, and making them identical with the Holy itself."[15] Thus, a symbol must "die to itself" and transcend its literal sense to affirm what it symbolizes. That is chiefly seen in the death of Jesus the Christ. In sum, Tillich's appeal to symbolic language is an expression of a *theologia crucis* that protects theology from idolatry and apophaticism.

God does not exist

Tillich's basic claim about God in ST1 is this: "God is the answer to the

---

14. Paul Tillich, *Theology of Culture* (New York: Oxford University Press, 1959), 67.
15. Ibid., 60.

question implied in being" (ST1, 163). However, notice what Tillich is *not* saying; he is not arguing that the existence of God might be *proven* by following the question of being up into God. In fact, he quite adamantly rejects the idea that God might be proven to exist in this way. That task misunderstands the nature of God as *ultimate*. Tillich provocatively suggests that God does not *exist*—at least not in the same way other finite beings exist. That is why it is problematic to try to "prove" that God exists, as if God could be subjected to a scientific method like proving the existence of atoms or the Pythagorean theorem. To prove that God exists in this way goes against Tillich's understanding of God as the ground and power of being-itself. It is vital to recognize the difference here.

Tillich argues that the classic "proofs" for the existence of God (the ontological and cosmological arguments) still have a place in theology, but they are not useful as arguments for God's *existence*. Instead, they express the *question* of God that is implied in finite being (ST1, 205). These proofs strive to overcome the limitations of finitude, but that is only possible through God's activity toward the finite; it is impossible to move in the other direction from the finite toward the infinite.

Tillich is a robust *theologian of grace* in this regard. God is not a being we might naturally reach through our own efforts, either intellectual or spiritual works. Instead, God's reality correlates with the questions implied in being. In other words, God *reaches us* in our situation of finitude; we do not work ourselves up to saving proof about God's being. Thus, when Tillich talks about the question implied in being, he correlates the reality of God with our situation to show that God is the answer to our situation of life under the conditions of finitude.

In this frame of mind, we might better understand Tillich's oft-quoted but frequently misunderstood claim:

> God does not exist. He is being-itself beyond essence and existence. Therefore, to argue that God exists is to deny him.[16]

This provocative statement is rooted in Tillich's conviction that God cannot be an object of human control. Of course, by speaking of God, God is unavoidably objectified according to the subject-object structure of

---

16. Paul Tillich, ST1, 205.

human speech, but nonetheless, the theologian must acknowledge and emphasize that God is not an object (ST1, 172-3). The symbol "God" is thus cruciform; it dies to itself to participate in what it indicates. That is what protects theology from the dual error of objectifying God with language or lapsing into silence and thus denying revelation. These points lead Tillich to argue that God does not *exist* because to exist would mean God becomes an object that human beings control. And so, while God *does* enter the structure of subject-object, God also transcends it.

With this context in mind, we can understand more charitably why Tillich argued that God "does not exist." The key to this is his definition of God as "being-itself beyond essence and existence" (ST1, 205). God transcends being while participating in it as its ground and power. That is simply another way of saying God is the creator. God is not a creature among other creatures—a being—and therefore, God does not "exist" but is beyond both essence and existence. God is the uncreated One. The language is philosophical, but Tillich's point is fundamentally biblical and relates to the doctrine of *creatio ex nihilo*, creation out of nothing. Creation does not exist on the same plane of being as the creator—this was the theological insight that doctrine underlined. Yet creation is also not conceived dualistically as if it were a reality entirely *set apart* from the creator. Thus, Tillich's solution to this dilemma is to argue that God is the ground and power of being, or being-itself. That is Tillich's fundamental definition of God. A God who is merely a being among others could not be an *ultimate* concern.

Tillich summarizes these points well:

> The being of God is being-itself. The being of God cannot be understood as the existence of a being alongside others or above others. If God is *a* being, he is subject to the categories of finitude, especially to space and substance. Even if he is called the "highest being" in the sense of the "most perfect" and the "most powerful" being, this situation is not changed. When applied to God, superlatives become diminutives. They place him on the level of other beings while elevating him above all of them.[17]

---

17. Paul Tillich, ST1, 235.

That is why Tillich suggests, "It is atheistic to affirm the existence of God as it is to deny it. God is being-itself, not *a* being" (ST1, 237). God is not subject to the structures of being, which are necessarily finite, because God is the ground of being. Symbolic language is necessary to protect this vital distinction.

For Tillich, only the statement that "God is being-itself is a nonsymbolic statement" (ST1, 238). Because it is a non-symbolic statement, this means "being-itself" refers directly to what it indicates; it does not point beyond itself. It also means that God as being-itself is foundational for all other statements about God, which are necessarily symbolic. Indeed, only because God is being-itself is God-talk possible. Why does Tillich make this argument? It is because of a doctrine known as the *analogia entis,* that is, the "analogy of being."

For Tillich, the analogy of being is what justifies our speech about God—indeed, it is the only way theology is humanly possible. The argument goes something like this: because our being is grounded in God, who is being-itself, then there is an *analogy* of being that makes God-talk possible. Therefore, finitude *can* speak of God because "that which is infinite is being-itself and because everything participates in being-itself" (ST1, 239). That also explains how true symbolic language about God participates in God. The claim that "God is being-itself" is non-symbolic is based on the analogy of being, that is, it is because all creation participates in God as the ground and power of being.

So far, all of this has been rather abstract. I want to explain these points more concretely by exploring Tillich's doctrine of God, particularly his exposition of the classic attributes of divine power, eternity, omnipresence, and omniscience. These doctrines take on a new and existentially relevant meaning because of Tillich's approach, resulting in a deeper recognition of the reality of God in the world.

God is Holy and Related

What I hope you are beginning to see about Tillich's doctrine of God is that it relies on a combination of divine *otherness* and *relatedness.* God is not an object we can approach like a human possession—God is non-objectifiable—yet God freely relates to human beings and wills to be known by us. Symbolic language reflects this basic point, that God is beyond essence and existence, yet God correlates with being because God is the ground and power of being-itself. In other words, *God is holy.*

Divine holiness expresses the "unapproachable character of God, or the impossibility of having a relation with [God] in the proper sense" (ST1, 271). That means God is "essentially holy" and therefore, "every relation with [God] involves the consciousness that it is paradoxical to be related to that which is holy" (ST1, 271). Because God is holy, every relation is at once affirmed and denied. It is affirmed in that human beings are "centered" selves "to whom every relation involves an object" (ST1, 271). In other words, to speak of God is always to objectify God. But this relation is also denied because God cannot become an object of human knowledge or action. God's holiness makes God's relatedness a paradox. God cannot be an object, yet God is the ground of creation and thus of every relation, which means God cannot be escaped.

It is perhaps helpful to see the Augustinian logic that is at work here. Tillich directly echoes Augustine by arguing that God is "nearer to the ego than the ego is to itself" as the creative ground of the creature (ST1, 271). Thus, Tillich once again retains both the ultimate and finite qualities of speaking about God's relation to the world. Symbolic speech about God is an attempt to navigate this paradox and faithfully uphold the holiness of God.

Tillich builds upon this basic premise and works out the various ways God relates to the world according to the classic categories of being. He avoids a common tendency among theologians to think abstractly about the so-called divine attributes by speaking of these symbols existentially.

OMNIPOTENCE

What does it mean to say that God is "all-powerful?" For Tillich, it is not that God is the highest power or the totality of power, but that God transcends and grounds the totality. Likewise, divine power is not merely the ability to do anything at will. Rather, Tillich writes, "God is the power of being, resisting and conquering nonbeing" (ST1, 272). This definition is primarily soteriological—thus, to say that God is all-powerful is to say God saves. For Tillich, this reflects the "Christian consciousness" that the "anxiety of nonbeing is eternally overcome in the divine life" (ST1, 273). That is, God almighty is a symbol that gives "the first and basic answer to the question implied in finitude" (ST1, 273).

In other words, to say that God is almighty is to declare that God overcomes nonbeing (death) and gives human beings the courage to participate in God's victory over nothingness. This confession does not remove the anxiety of nonbeing, but rather, God as the power of being is the basis for the courage to resist nonbeing. Grace is, for Tillich, the courage to affirm being (to accept yourself) despite the threat of nonbeing (despite being unacceptable) because God almighty is the power of being that overcomes nonbeing (because God saves and heals).

Sunday school children learn the concept of omnipotence in a way that portrays God as akin to Superman, the ultimate power among others. That is why difficulties often arise about God's action in the world (or lack of action), especially in the face of suffering—that is, the classic theodicy dilemma: If God is good and all-powerful, why is there suffering?

Tillich's reworking of the doctrine of omnipotence is a helpful move away from this speculative tendency. Divine power is, instead, defined here as the power to affirm existence despite the threat of nonbeing. God is not Superman. God is the power of being and the basis for resisting nonbeing. The reality that God is omnipotent grounds the *courage* to face nonbeing as finite creatures.

Eternity

Similarly, Tillich removes divine eternity from the realm of speculation by refusing to define eternity as endless time or timelessness. Like omnipotence, divine eternity is the basis for "the courage to endure the anxiety of temporal existence" (ST1, 274). The symbol of God's eternity reflects God's power to conquer "the nonbeing of temporality" (ST1, 274). Thus, God transcends time yet also embraces time: "Since time is created in the ground of the divine life, God is essentially related to it" (ST1, 274).

We often place eternity in opposition to time. However, Tillich suggests that the symbol of divine eternity reflects at once the embrace of temporality and the transcendence of it, thus providing the basis for courage to overcome the anxiety of temporality.

Tillich argues that eternity "must first be symbolized as an eternal present" (ST1, 275). That means the movement "from past to future without ceasing to be present" (ST1, 275). Tillich then explains the existential meaning of divine eternity: "Faith in the eternal God is the basis for a courage which conquers the negativities of the temporal process" (ST1, 276). Hope in eternal life is based on the divine victory over the nonbeing of temporality; God lives in the eternal present. Thus, faith in the eternal God produces courage in the face of the temporal threat of nonbeing.

Omnipresence

Tillich also criticizes any concept of divine omnipresence that suggests God extends endlessly in space or exists without a definite space, that is, spacelessness. The former claim is pantheist, and the latter is deistic (ST1, 277). In other words, a God whose being extends endlessly is identical with space itself, while a God without definite space transcends space without participating in it. Both concepts are empty and irrelevant to our lives. In contrast, Tillich holds together the divine relation to space with the divine transcendence of space in a way that sparks courage to face the anxiety of space. So, Tillich defines omnipresence as God's "creative participation in the spatial existence of [God's] creatures" (ST1, 277).

The meaning of God's relation to space is that divine omnipresence "overcomes the anxiety of not having space for one's self" (ST1, 278), which inspires the courage to accept the limitations and anxieties of spatial existence. A spatial paradox marks our existence: "we are always at home and not at home" (ST1, 278). That is, we are "always in the sanctuary," even amid the secular (ST1, 278). The experience of omnipresence "breaks down the difference between the sacred and the profane" (ST1, 278). Omnipresence overcomes the threat of nonbeing in relation to the spatial reality of finitude. God transcends space while participating in it. God makes space for finitude.

Omniscience

To say that God is omniscient is not to suggest that God simply knows the most. Rather, divine omniscience is a symbol that expresses, "Nothing is outside the centered unity of [God's] life; nothing is strange, dark, hidden, isolated, unapproachable" (ST1, 279). Because God is the ground of being, there is nothing that exists outside of the "logos structure of being" (ST1, 279). The very structures of reality are grounded in the knowledge of God. That is, God not only knows all things but also grounds the knowledge of all things. God participates in the logos structure of knowledge yet transcends, and is therefore, not subject to its limitations.

Existentially, this means that nothing is hidden from God's spiritual life. Thus, "the anxiety of the dark and the hidden is overcome in the faith of the divine omniscience" (ST1, 279). Omniscience further means the "logical... foundation of the belief in the openness of reality to human knowledge" (ST1, 279). In other words, our very knowledge of created reality is possible because "we participate in divine knowledge" (ST1, 279). Finitude knows reality and is not inherently limited to ignorance because of the power to overcome ignorance through divine knowledge is present. Human beings can and do participate in the truth despite their finitude. We at once experience the limitations of finitude yet are not restricted by ultimate meaninglessness.

Tillich reframes these classic attributes to show how God is the answer to the question implied in being, which suggests the existential immediacy of God's relation to the world. God is not defined as the highest among other beings but as the ground of being, whom we speak of symbolically as omnipotent (powerful to overcome nonbeing), eternal (powerful to overcome the nonbeing of temporality), omnipresent (powerful to overcome spatial nonbeing), and omniscient (powerful to overcome ignorance). Tillich's doctrine of God thus produces the courage to resist nonbeing, a courage grounded in the God who overcomes. It is a drastic move away from the speculative tendencies that often plague discussions about the attributes of God.

The strength of Tillich's approach is that he thinks God meets us where we actually are, not in the realm of theoretical speculation, but concretely where life happens. God is existentially relevant to human beings.

Christian faith in God as the ground and power of being is a deeply existential faith. It is not about mindlessly accepting a set of confessions that bear no meaning for real life. Rather, to confess God is to *trust* in God as the power of being, as the one who overcomes finite limitations because God is not one being among others but the ground and power of being. Trust in this God is not speculative or abstract—like trust in Superman—but existential and produces the courage to be despite the threat of nonbeing. God is deeply and genuinely related to the world while being the transcendent power that overcomes the limitations of finitude. Only such a God deserves our trust as an ultimate concern, that is, with our whole self.

God is Love

Tillich turns from the classical attributes of God to examine the biblical claim that "God is love." Tillich writes that love is "an ontological concept" (ST1, 279). Therefore, he applies the concept of God as being-itself to suggest that being-itself *is* love. But Tillich is quick to clarify that this statement is meaningless unless love is properly defined. For Tillich, "love" is "every life-process [that] unites a trend toward separation with a trend toward reunion. The unbroken unity of these two trends is the ontological nature of love" (ST1, 279). In another essay, Tillich defines love as the "moving power of life." It is "the drive towards the unity of the separated."[18]

Tillich further explains love in terms of *libido* (the fulfillment of need), *philia* (the desire for friendship), *eros* (the desire to move from lower to higher), and finally, *agape*, which best describes God's nature as love. Tillich writes, "*Agapē* accepts the other in spite of resistance. It suffers and forgives. It seeks the personal fulfilment of the other" (ST1, 280). It is thus the ultimate unity of lover and beloved, and the best description of God's nature.

However, Tillich gives space for applying the other concepts of love to God because devotional language uses them metaphorically: God is *libido* means God longs for the creature; God is *philia* means the friendship of equals, which Christ speaks about in John 15:15; God is *eros* means the eschatological movement that drives toward God becoming "all in all." Yet only *agape* captures the love that God is without qualifications.

---

18. Paul Tillich, *Love, Power, and Justice* (New York: Oxford University Press, 1954), p. 25.

Because God is the ground and power of being-itself, and being-itself is love, then finite being loves with the love that *is* God. Tillich comments, "The trinitarian distinctions (separation and reunion) makes it possible to speak of divine self-love" (ST1, 282). Thus, our love for God includes the reality that we could not love God without loving God *with* God's love; in other words, "God is a subject even where he seems to be an object" (ST1, 282). Our love of God is not generated independently without the love that God is. Thus, love is not another *work* but a gift of the divine life, a gift of grace.

The concept of divine self-love also has profound implications for human self-love. In contrast with Calvin—who excluded the possibility of self-love from the Christian life and nearly succeeded in turning self-hatred into a Christian virtue—Tillich thinks that God's trinitarian self-love analogously and indirectly points to a "divinely demanded human self-love" (ST1, 282). That point relates to Tillich's refrain that grace means accepting oneself in spite of being unacceptable (see the sermon attached to the next chapter). Thus, self-love is *necessary*.[19] Yet Tillich stresses that this concept of self-love needs to include *agape*, or it risks becoming selfish. True self-love means loving ourselves "as the eternal image of the divine life" (ST1, 282). But Tillich helpfully provides theological grounding for self-love, and thereby condemns the religious justifications of self-hatred. Tillich is emphatic on this point: there is nothing spiritually beneficial in hating yourself.

Tillich's ontological definition of love implies that the very structure of creation is oriented around the love that unites with the estranged. That leads to an essential pattern in Tillich's system: union-estrangement-reunion. This pattern will be central to the next chapter, when we consider Tillich's christology. But it is worth noticing its centrality in his doctrine of God. Because God is love, being-itself is a love that reunites the estranged.

---

19. In 1954, three years after ST1 was published, Tillich slightly amended this endorsement of self-love, mostly due to semantic difficulties. The term "self-love" is a *metaphor* that can be clarified by speaking of "self-affirmation" or "self-acceptance." Self-love requires reunification of what's separated, which makes it a difficult concept to uphold meaningfully. That is why Tillich calls human self-love *analogous* to divine self-love. See *Love, Power, and Justice* (New York: Oxford University Press, 1954), 33-34.

Love and Justice

Tillich emphasizes the unity of love and justice for both God and society. He defines justice as "that side of love which affirms the independent right of object and subject within the love relation" (ST1, 282). Love preserves the freedom of the beloved. But it is not freedom in terms of separation, but the affirmation of uniqueness. Tillich captures this paradox well: "It neither forces [humanity into fulfillment] nor leaves" (ST1, 283). That is, justice is the side of love that acknowledges freedom while also compelling the beloved toward reunion. However, at the same time, justice involves resistance and condemnation. Tillich is careful not to separate love and justice, and his description of divine wrath helpfully explains how this unity is possible.

Divine wrath is directed against "that which violates love" (ST1, 283). It is not arbitrary wrath but the wrath *of love*. Tillich writes, "Condemnation is not the negation of love but the negation of the negation of love" (ST1, 283). So while justice involves an affirmation of freedom, it also condemns whatever separates the lover and beloved. If that were not the case, if love is merely affirmation without any condemnation of that which violates love, it would permit the destruction of love. Instead, that which threatens love must be given over to its own self-destruction. Justice negates the negations of love. Thus, divine wrath is a *function* of love, not its opposite. The "wrath of God" is not an arbitrary expression of divine anger but reveals God's love for the beloved, a love that must overcome that which threatens love.

That leads Tillich to consider grace, which is "The divine love in relation to the unjust creature" (ST1, 285). God accepts what is unacceptable. God's acceptance of the creature thus depends solely on God. But there also exists what Tillich calls "providential grace," which is the preparatory grace known classically as "prevenient grace." So, what do we do with the fact that not everyone is prepared to accept divine grace?

That leads to the question of predestination. Tillich rejects "double" predestination or any claim that God desires the destruction of some creatures. That "violates both the divine love and the divine power. Ontologically, eternal condemnation is a contradiction in terms" (ST1, 285). Why? Because eternal condemnation gives *ultimate* validity to evil, which introduces a dualistic split within being-itself, i.e., God.

In contrast, Tillich defines predestination as "providence with respect to one's ultimate destiny" (ST1, 286). It should not be confused with determinism, wherein all events in history are predetermined. Instead, predestination is related to *ultimate* destiny. That further means, for Tillich, that God's relation to the creature is always understood symbolically wherein "the categories are affirmed and negated at the same time" (ST1, 286). Thus, predestination cannot be taken literally in the sense of pre-determining all that takes place in time. Rather, "the word must be taken in the symbolic sense of pointing to the existential experience that, in relation to God, God's act always precedes and, further, that, in order to be certain of one's fulfilment, one can and must look at God's activity alone" (ST1, 286). Therefore, predestination is "the highest affirmation of the divine love" (ST1, 286). It is the affirmation that God acts towards creation graciously.

A key passage from this section on love and predestination reveals an important insight about the christological foundation of Tillich's theology; he writes:

> The divine love is the final answer to the question implied in human existence, including finitude, the threat of disruption, and estrangement. Actually this answer is given only in the manifestation of the divine love under the conditions of existence. It is the christological answer to which the doctrine of the divine love gives the systematic foundation, although one would not be able to speak of this foundation without having received the christological answer. But what is existentially first may be systematically last and vice versa. That is also true of the doctrine of the trinity.[20]

The question of being is ultimately answered by the doctrine that God is love. Therefore, it could be argued that Tillich's correlation method is essentially the correlation of the love of God with the human situation; it is a theological method rooted in the actuality of divine love. Furthermore, the reality that Jesus is the Christ is the foundation of this doctrine. While his method requires first considering the existential situation, Tillich directly states here that the question is not what is first systemati-

---

20. Paul Tillich, ST1, 286.

cally, even if it is first existentially. Instead, the most foundational doctrine, for Tillich, is that Jesus is the Christ who manifests the New Being, which is how we know that God is love.

What this passage also clues us in on is that Tillich has not been speculating about God's love aimlessly. Rather, he is talking about divine love as it is revealed and founded upon the reality of Jesus as the Christ. This point is important to acknowledge because it suggests that Tillich is profoundly christological, despite the mistaken claim that he argues purely philosophically.

In the next chapter, we will more directly consider Tillich's christology, which will give me a chance to discuss some of the important questions that this section has raised, namely, the questions of salvation and hell. But for now, this passage indicates that Tillich's reflection on God's love is rooted in his doctrine of Christ.

Lord and Father

Tillich concludes volume one by reflecting on God's power and love through the symbols Lord and Father. He writes, "While Lord is basically the expression of man's relation to the God who is holy power, Father is basically the expression of man's relation to the God who is holy love" (ST1, 287). The Lordship of God articulates distance, while the term Father claims a unity. Both are necessary for speaking about God, but these terms are symbolic, not literal. God is not a Lord like the lords of feudal history; nor is God a male, as the term Father implies. Thus, these symbols are another helpful example for understanding what Tillich means by symbolic speech about God.

The symbols Lord and Father point beyond themselves and participate in the reality to which they point. These were Tillich's first two definitions of symbolic language. These symbols not only open up levels of reality that would have been unapproachable otherwise but also unlock dimensions about ourselves. Thus, the symbols Lord and Father open up something profound about God's power and love, while also opening up a reality about what it means to be human, to rule and parent one another well.

These two symbols grew from an individual or collective unconscious —social power was expressed by lordship, and personal love was located with fatherhood—but Tillich notes how they have today become stumbling blocks. Theologians must be sensitive to this fact. Recall Tillich's sixth point about symbols: they can grow and die. Tillich only lived to see the beginnings of feminist and anti-colonial theory, but he would probably have recognized how these changes in society might lead to the death of the classic symbols of Lord and Father. That does not mean the end of talking about God's power and love. Instead, it means the development of new symbolic God-talk that is no longer a stumbling block but an aid that fulfills the first four requirements of symbolic language. The church and theology are still trying to work out this difficulty today, though many have tried to find alternative language around the power and love of God free from the history of problematic lordship (colonial dominance) and fatherhood (patriarchy). Tillich's concept of symbolic God-talk can be (and has been) a fruitful contribution to this conversation.

Conclusion: a note on "existentialism"

Tillich's doctrine of God is remarkably relevant to human life. And that is precisely his goal. By correlating the message of God with the existential reality of finite being, Tillich shows that "God is the answer to the question implied in being" (ST1, 163). The answer "God" is not projected or defined from the question; rather, the question itself is only possible because of the presence of the answer, because God is the ground and power of being. Tillich is clear that the content of the Christian message "cannot be derived from the questions" of the situation (ST1, 64). Instead, "revelation is presupposed in all parts of the system as the ultimate source of the contents of the Christian faith" (ST1, 67-8).

I will return to this point in chapter five, but it is worth briefly noting what this means. Simply put, Tillich's procedure is not a movement from below to above. Tillich emphasizes, "All theological statements are existential; they imply the man who makes the statement or who asks the question" (ST1, 269). That means theology cannot operate as if it speaks of God in a vacuum apart from the person speaking, from their language and culture, existential concerns, anxieties, and fears, and the structures of being and existence. But it does *not* mean that these existential questions are the foundation of the theological answer, which Tillich insists can only be given by revelation.

So, Tillich's doctrine of God is deeply existential because of his conviction that theology itself is unavoidably existential. However, the term "existentialism" can be confusing. To clarify it, consider how Tillich defines existentialism:

> Existential is what characterizes our real existence in all its concreteness, in all its accidental elements, in its freedom and responsibility, in its failure, and in its separation from its true and essential being. Theology thinks on the basis of this existential situation and in continuous relation to it. Asking for the meaning of being, theology asks for the ultimate ground and power and norm and aim of being.... In other words: In asking for the meaning of being, theology asks for God.[21]

Tillich's doctrine of God is existential in *this* sense: it deals with the real existence of human beings in their anxious situation of finitude. Tillich's basic point is this: we cannot jump over our own shadow; therefore, all theology must incorporate the existential questions of being.

Theologians sometimes treat the doctrine of God as if it were a philosophical thought experiment or a speculative game. Tillich's doctrine of God is noteworthy for its insistence upon the existential significance of God for human life, that God is *our* God, the ground and power of being. Such a God is properly known as the object of our ultimate concern, of faith. That is because such a God is worth risking our very being on; we can trust God with our entire mind and heart.

We should carefully distinguish between *a theology that is existential* and *existential theology*. Tillich's theology is best understood as the former, not the latter. In 1960, Tillich reflected on his attempt to "unite these two lines," namely, the "essentialist line and... the existentialist line."[22] Tillich is convinced that the essentialist and existentialist lines of thought need to be correlated. No one can produce a purely essentialist or existentialist theology. He writes, "Sometimes I have been called an 'existentialist philosopher', or better, an 'existentialist theologian'. But there is no such

---

21. Paul Tillich, *The Protestant Era*, trans. James Luther Adams (Chicago: The University of Chicago Press, 1948), 88.
22. Paul Tillich, "Philosophical Background of my Theology" in *Main Works / Hauptwerke* vol. 1, ed. Herausgegeben von Carl Heinz Ratschow (Berlin: De Gruyter, 1989), 416.

thing..."[23] Why? Because "existentialism raises the problems of human existence; and theology... tries to give answers..."[24] But the answers theology gives must make use of existentialist philosophy. Therefore, Tillich is arguing for the mutual dependence of both existentialist philosophy and essentialist theology.

Theologians throughout history have always made use of philosophical concepts, depending on the historical situation. However, Tillich is quick to add that "if there is philosophy used in theology, this does not mean that theology is dependent on any special philosophical system."[25] Philosophy is an unavoidable conversation partner of theology.

The point in stressing all this is to show that Tillich's doctrine of God makes use of existential concepts, but it is *not* beholden to existentialism as such. Therefore, it is wrong to label Tillich an "existentialist" theologian. Instead, Tillich attempts to be at once a philosopher and theologian: "As a theologian I have tried to remain a philosopher, and vice versa."[26] Tillich's fidelity to the unity of the theological answer and the philosophical question, of God and being, is deeply incarnational. His doctrine of God is best understood within this framework. God, the ground and power of being, is the answer to the question implied in the anxiety of being finite and human.

---

23. Ibid.
24. Ibid.
25. Ibid., 420.
26. Paul Tillich, *On the Boundary* (New York: Charles Scribner's Sons, 1966), 58.

Sermon: Escape from God

God as the "ground and power of being" implies the inescapability of God. That is because all who exist participate in being-itself. God is the one in whom all creation lives and moves and has its being (Acts 17:28). Only an inescapable God is truly God. In a sermon on Psalm 139—"Where could I go from thy spirit, and where could I flee from Thy Face?"—Tillich comments on the inescapability of God but also on our paradoxical desire to flee from God.

Indeed, the inescapability of God is something deeply terrifying for us. A God we might escape from is a God of our own making, who could be kept at a safe distance. Tillich identifies this tension in the psalmist: by acknowledging that God cannot be escaped, the writer also recognizes the desire to escape God. That leads Tillich to suggest that "a man who has never tried to flee God has never experienced the God Who is really God."[1] This point seems contradictory, but Tillich explains:

> When I speak of God I do not refer to the many gods of our own making, the gods with whom we can live rather comfortably. For there is no reason to flee a god who is the perfect picture of every-

---

1. Paul Tillich, *The Shaking of the Foundations* (New York: Charles Scribner's Sons, 1948), 42.

thing that is good in man. Why try to escape from such a far-removed ideal? And there is no reason to flee from a god who is simply the universe, or the laws of nature, or the course of history.... There is no reason to flee from a god who is nothing more than a benevolent father, a father who guarantees our immortality and final happiness. Why try to escape from someone who serves us so well? No, those are not pictures of God, but rather of man, trying to make God in his own image and for his own comfort. They are the products of man's imagination and wishful thinking, justly denied by every honest atheist. A god whom we can easily bear, a god from whom we do not have to hide, a god whom we do not hate in moments, a god whose destruction we never desire, is not God at all, and has no reality.[2]

Tillich's vision of God is far from shallow. A watered-down reading of his doctrine of God might lead to a vision of God as merely the processes of nature or the guarantor of happiness. But Tillich does not accept a *safe* God. Instead, he wrestles with God like Jacob, protests like Job, and cries out from the depths of despair and anxiety. And only from this wrestling does God become truly relevant to our humanity. If God were merely the negation of our doubts, fears, and insecurities, God would be a magic genie. But the God who is truly God is a God to struggle with, against, and for. It is not because God is *against* us that we wrestle with God—it is precisely because God is so thoroughly *for us*. God's inescapable *nearness* is what causes us to flee from God. The inescapability of grace, of God's nearness, leads to the escape from God.

Notice how this paradox embraces human protesting against a domesticated God, like the protests often found in atheism. Tillich discusses the "honest atheists" and suggests that they are justified in their denial of a domesticated God. Indeed, Tillich's vision of God not only embraces protest against God but makes it essential. He comments, "The first step to atheism is always a theology which drags God down to the level of doubtful things."[3] Theology that takes God seriously *as God* embraces the protest of atheism, and it stands shoulder to shoulder in rejecting every

---

2. Ibid.
3. Ibid., 45.

false, domesticated god. Protest is not always a sign of rebellion, but can often mean we have truly engaged the God who is ultimate, not merely a safe projection of our wishful thinking. Tillich writes:

> [M]an cannot stand the God Who is really God. Man tries to escape God, and hates Him, because he cannot escape Him. The protest against God, the will that there be no God, and the flight to atheism are all genuine elements of profound religion. And only on the basis of these elements has religion meaning and power.[4]

Protest is a genuine element in religion. Cheap faiths, cheap concepts of God, suppress this protest. A Christian faith that is so *fragile* that it must suppress all wrestling and doubting is not faith at all but empty fanaticism. Faith is not faith if it does not embrace and concern us ultimately, as a risk for which we stake our entire being. Only the God who is truly God is the object of ultimate concern. A faith that cannot embrace protest, doubt, and despair is shallow.

This vision of God sounds paradoxical at first, but it is vital to see how it is connected to Tillich's driving concern about a God who is profoundly related to the human situation. Such a God cannot be an "object" we either accept or reject casually. The true God is the One for whom we risk our entire being. The classical doctrine of omnipotence lacks this dimension of existential concern, but that is precisely what Tillich hopes to recover. His suggestion, which is central to not only this sermon but his entire theological project, is that these concepts must be rediscovered for our time. "Let us therefore forget these concepts, *as* concepts, and try to find their genuine meaning within our own experience."[5] This statement could very well function as a summary of much of Tillich's theology.

We should not misunderstand Tillich here. This is not an attempt to *reduce* Christian symbols to our level. Instead, it is based on a deep conviction that God is truly related to the human situation, that God is actively involved in our lives. Therefore, the omnipresence of God, or any other doctrine, must be rediscovered according to its genuine meaning

---

4. Ibid., 45.
5. Ibid., 46.

within experience. It is clear, from this sermon, that Tillich is sensitive to how God is both a source of comfort and a challenge. He altogether rejects the problematic ways we sometimes make God merely a tool in our own self-comfort. A God who is truly God is both a comfort and a challenge because such a God is worth staking our very being upon.

Omnipresence is terrifying because it means nothing is ultimately hidden. We will be held to account for every secret thought and act. "Omnipresence means that our privacy is public."[6] While Tillich does not press this point, there are profound political implications behind this insight. Consider those who suffer from injustices done in secret, where the perpetrator gets away with the wrong they have committed. Divine omnipresence, in this sense, is a promise that all will come to light, that God is present and knows the victim's suffering. And God will make right the wrongs that were done. This application is not Tillich's point exactly, but it does help explain how the inescapability of God can be something terrifying but also liberating. For the victims of history, it is liberating; for their oppressors, it is terrifying.

Finally, Tillich concludes his sermon by commenting on how the psalmist overcomes the tension between the inescapable God and our desire to flee God:

> The psalmist has overcome his wavering between the will to flee God and the will to be equal with God. He has found that the final solution lies in the fact that the Presence of the Witness, the Presence of the centre of all life within the centre of *his* life, implies both a radical attack on his existence, and the ultimate meaning of his existence. We are known in a depth of darkness through which we ourselves do not even dare to look. And at the same time, we are seen in a height of a fullness which surpasses our highest vision. That infinite tension is the atmosphere in which religion lives.[7]

The human situation is found in this unavoidable tension. We are *known*—truly and deeply and terrifyingly known—in the depth of our

---

6. Ibid.
7. Ibid., 50.

being. Yet we are also placed in the fullness of New Being. We are accepted in spite of being unacceptable. We believe, yet we need help with our unbelief. We try to flee from the inescapable God. To be human is to live in this tension.

Sidebar: The Courage to Be

One of Tillich's most popular books—*The Courage to Be*—was a series of lectures given at Yale University on anxiety, courage, and God. He analyzes how the anxiety over the threat of nonbeing is intrinsic to what it means to be human. Courage means accepting this anxiety: "The question of God is the question of the possibility of this courage" (ST1, 198). So the question of God and the concept of courage are closely related in Tillich's theology. This sidebar will examine Tillich's lecture in connection with his doctrine of God and divine grace.

Three types of anxiety

Tillich examines courage both as an ethical and ontological reality. Courage is ontological because it involves "the universal and essential self-affirmation of one's being..."[1] And it is ethical in the sense that courage itself is "the ethical act in which man affirms his own being in spite of those elements of his existence which conflict with his essential self-affirmation."[2] Thus, the ontological and ethical are related.

Tillich defines courage as "self-affirmation *'in-spite-of'*... that which

---

1. Paul Tillich, *The Courage to Be* (New Haven: Yale University Press, 1952), 3.
2. Ibid.

tends to prevent the self from affirming itself."[3] The "in spite of" character of courage is essential to what it means to be human and live with the anxieties of finitude. Being exists with the perpetual threat of nonbeing, which is the source of our anxiety. Tillich then analyzes the three forms of anxiety: anxiety of death, anxiety of meaninglessness, and the anxiety of condemnation.[4]

The first form involves the awareness of one's finitude and the biological reality of death. This anxiety is always present in the experience of time and relates to the concept of fate. Tillich writes, "Man as man in every civilization is anxiously aware of the threat of nonbeing and needs the courage to affirm himself in spite of it."[5] Consciously or not, every human act takes place within time and thus within the limitations of finitude, which induces the anxiety of death.

The second form involves the anxiety of an empty existence, that is, a life without meaning. It is the loss of an ultimate concern, which gives life its spiritual center. Whereas the threat of nonbeing in biological life expresses itself through fate in the anxiety of death, this category involves the threat of nonbeing to spiritual life, expressed in emptiness and loss.[6] In this connection, Tillich's concept of faith and doubt comes back into the discussion.

The desire to live free from doubt, from the threat of meaninglessness, is an attempt to escape this anxiety. But to doubt is human, and the suppression of this doubt is dehumanizing. That is why faith is an existential risk: it involves risking the meaning of one's life on an ultimate concern. This anxiety leads some to avoid the risk of faith altogether (or at least attempt to) by excluding all doubt, but this means becoming enslaved to a dogma. But whether it is an infallible book, person, or tradition that takes the place of one's ultimate concern, it is a false ultimate (an idol). This desire to avoid doubt and the anxiety of meaninglessness is also a foundation of fundamentalism (which Tillich calls fanaticism).

Fundamentalism is the suppression of all doubt, anxiously avoiding the inevitable risk of faith in order to protect it from the threat of meaninglessness. The fundamentalist must then suppress doubt in others

---

3. Ibid., 32.
4. Ibid., 41.
5. Ibid., 43.
6. Ibid., 48.

through dogmatic attacks against "heretics" and "doubters," but that is because they must first suppress doubt in themselves. This attempt is never fully successful. Doubt is an unavoidable part of faith's risk. But Tillich connects here more concretely the risk of faith with the courage that affirms one's spiritual meaning (ultimate concern) in spite of the threat of meaninglessness (of a false ultimate). Fundamentalism avoids this anxiety unsuccessfully by trading faith for unquestioning belief in dogma. But it is idolatrous to make a finite object or person into an ultimate concern.

Finally, there is the anxiety of guilt and the fear of condemnation, which is the ultimate threat of nonbeing. This category involves the classic concepts of sin and guilt; it expresses the threat of nonbeing upon the *moral* life. For Tillich, "The moral imperative is the command to become what one potentially is, a *person* within a community of persons."[7] With this, Tillich is describing moral acts as the fulfillment of our essential being. But because human beings are also *free,* they never fulfill their essential being perfectly. Thus, there is an unavoidable guilt surrounding the issue of what a person makes of themselves in existence with the potentialities of their essence. In other words, human beings are *responsible* for their moral selves, and that leads to the anxiety of guilt. That encapsulates the threat of nonbeing upon our moral life.

Courage or despair

Tillich is emphatic that courage does not *remove* anxiety. "Since anxiety is existential, it cannot be removed. But courage takes the anxiety of nonbeing into itself. Courage is self-affirmation 'in spite of,' namely in spite of nonbeing."[8] The threats of death, meaninglessness, and guilt are essential to what it is to be human. They describe the "in-spite-of" character of being that threatens the affirmation of being. But anxiety can also give way to despair. For Tillich, each human being lives between the choice of courage or despair.

With this in mind, Tillich analyzes what happens when we choose despair and not courage. In the realm of biological anxiety over death, the

---

7. Paul Tillich, *Morality and Beyond* (New York: Harper & Row, 1963), 19.
8. Paul Tillich, *The Courage to Be* (New Haven: Yale University Press, 1952), 66.

individual will choose *security* instead of the courage that is required for full self-affirmation. Security is not always a bad thing, but it becomes unhealthy and pathological when it is a pathway for avoiding the courage of affirmation in spite of the threat of death. Every person will eventually lose their health, their friends and family, and their material possessions. No quantity or quality of medicine, relationships, or wealth can make up for that fact. Sometimes despair looks like barricading one's self from the dangers of life. But it is despair nonetheless to choose safety over the risks of self-affirmation.

In the realm of spiritual anxiety over meaninglessness, the individual will choose *dogmas* and *systems* instead of the risks of courage. "Existential anxiety of doubt," writes Tillich, "drives the person toward the creation of certitude in systems of meaning, which are supported by tradition and authority."[9] That was analyzed above as fundamentalism. But even a liberal theologian can lose courage by creating an unquestionable dogma for themselves with their philosophy, ideology, etc. Courage in this context means risking one's very being on an ultimate concern that transcends all systems, ideas, structures, or dogmas. It is, in other terms, faith in the transcendent God, who is no being among others but the ground and power of being. No human philosophy or theology can be equated with the God who refuses to become an idol.

In the realm of moral anxiety over guilt and condemnation, the individual must choose between the courage of grace *or* salvation by works through behavior modification. Tillich does not directly use this language, but it is implied in his analysis. The anxiety of guilt leads us to avoid guilt through self-discipline toward the goal of moral perfection.[10] The individual is, however, aware that these acts cannot remove estrangement; we are not existentially what our essential being is meant to be (moral imperative). Thus, the moral situation is one in which guilt is avoided, but it also means giving up the freedom of responsible decisions. The guilt is *repressed*, but it cannot be removed. Moralism and behavior modification cannot cover up the anxiety of guilt.

Tillich analyzes this situation of anxiety to show how courage is an act of *grace*. The "courage to be" is not and cannot be a *command* imposed

---

9. Ibid., 76.
10. Ibid., 75.

Sidebar: The Courage to Be

upon us arbitrarily. "Religiously speaking, it is a matter of grace."[11] Tillich goes on to analyze various forms of courage, doubt, anxiety, and despair. He comments on the situation of our age (speaking about the mid-twentieth century) as one of anxiety over doubt and a loss of meaning, which Auden called the "age of anxiety." Ultimately, Tillich points to courage as grace because it is not something that human beings might generate for themselves, being bound by their anxieties. Rather, courage requires a power and ground that transcends while incorporating the threat of nonbeing. This is where Tillich's analysis of courage begins to overlap with his doctrine of salvation, which we will consider more fully in the next chapter. We will still conclude, however, by identifying how Tillich connects courage and the anxiety of being with divine grace.

Grace

Finite being cannot overcome the threats of nonbeing and the anxiety of death, meaninglessness, and condemnation. That is why, for Tillich, courage requires a transcendent ground and power. It requires *grace*. "The courage which takes this threefold anxiety into itself," he explains, "must be rooted in a power of being that is greater than the power of oneself and the power of one's world."[12] Courage means affirming one's being despite the threat of nonbeing. But such an act of courage always has "an open or hidden religious root. For religion is the state of being grasped by the power of being-itself."[13] This religious dimension of courage leads to a theological answer to the question implied in being.

Tillich's concept of courage has profound soteriological overtones. It is not by working ourselves up into courage that we live courageously. Rather, Tillich writes, "one can become confident about one's existence only after ceasing to base one's confidence on oneself.... It is based on God and solely on God..."[14] Because courage is based upon the ground and power of being, not on the self, it is a religious courage, whether its transcendent element is acknowledged or not. Therefore, Tillich describes

---

11. Ibid., 85.
12. Ibid., 155.
13. Ibid., 156.
14. Ibid., 163.

the courage to be in religious terms, but at once, in deeply existential terms.

Tillich employs the doctrine of justification by grace to describe "the courage to be" as "the courage to accept oneself as accepted in spite of being unacceptable."[15] That is his attempt at a modern interpretation of the justification of the unjust sinner in the age of anxiety. This courage is the "victory over the anxiety of guilt and condemnation…"[16] This courage does not deny guilt but risks accepting the acceptance of grace despite unacceptability. If the law speaks a word of unacceptability, of guilt and condemnation, which expresses the threat of nonbeing morally, then the gospel speaks a clear and decisive word of acceptance. The courage to be is to accept acceptance in spite of being unacceptable. That courage is grounded in the God who forgives and justifies sinners. The anxiety of guilt is overcome by the power of grace, by accepting acceptance.

This radical act of self-affirmation in spite of the anxiety of guilt is Tillich's modern phrase for the justification of sinners. It is the gospel translated into terms relevant and immediately existential for modern people struggling under the weight and anxiety of estrangement: *You are accepted.* Therefore, God is the power that "heals by accepting the unacceptable…. The acceptance of God, his forgiving and justifying act, is the only and ultimate source of a courage to be which is able to take the anxiety of guilt and condemnation into itself."[17]

The anxieties of death and meaninglessness are also met with grace. The anxiety of death is connected to fate and time, but the message of providence and participation in God's life produces the courage to be in spite of the threat of nonbeing. "Providence," explains Tillich, "is the religious symbol of the courage of confidence with respect to fate and death."[18] This courage takes the anxiety of death into itself and affirms being in spite of it. Tillich also comments on the popular belief in the "immortality of the soul." He rejects this idea as unchristian. It is a "poor symbol for the courage to be in the face of one's having to die."[19] It offers a cheap hope and answer to the anxiety of death. Instead, Tillich argues

---

15. Ibid., 164.
16. Ibid.
17. Ibid., 166.
18. Ibid., 168.
19. Ibid., 169.

that a better foundation for the courage to be is the state of being "accepted into communion with God..."[20]

For Tillich, the threats of anxiety and nonbeing are not destroyed through courage; instead, courage must incorporate these threats yet go on "in spite of" them. The "in spite of" character is essential. That is why the doctrine of an immortal soul is inadequate—it suppresses the real anxiety over death. Theories of immortality suppress but do not answer the anxieties of death in a similar way that doubt is suppressed by adherence to dogmatic belief instead of the courageous risk of faith. Courage does not avoid death but takes it into itself and affirms being in spite of nonbeing. In contrast, the immortality of the soul removes the "in spite of" that is central for every courageous self-affirmation. Therefore, Tillich suggests thinking of eternity in terms of our being accepted into communion with God because the one "who participates in God participates in eternity."[21] Accepting the acceptance of God—that is, grace—is the foundation for the courage to be.

The anxiety of meaninglessness is answered by the reality of faith, which is the state of being grasped by the power of being-itself. In that regard, Tillich writes:

> The courage to be is an expression of faith and what 'faith' means must be understood through the courage to be. We have defined courage as the self-affirmation of being in spite of nonbeing. The power of this self-affirmation is the power of being which is effective in every act of courage. Faith is the experience of this power.[22]

He further explains that faith is the "existential acceptance of something transcending my ordinary experience."[23] As we have discussed, this means that faith is not a matter of opinions or ideas but of being grasped by the power of being-itself. The connecting point, for Tillich, is that faith, as this state of being grasped, is what makes possible the self-affirmation that is necessary for courage. In short, "faith is the basis of the

---

20. Ibid., 170.
21. Ibid.
22. Ibid., 172.
23. Ibid., 173.

courage to be."[24] Faith is then a meaningful act because it involves being grasped by an ultimate concern. And in that regard, it is the answer to the question implied by the anxiety of meaninglessness.

What Tillich has done in this book, then, is to analyze our existential situation and correlate it with the answer provided by the Christian message. Yet he applies that message in a way that is powerfully relevant to the situation of anxiety. This move is further confirmation of Tillich's deeply incarnational theology, that God's reality fully meets us.

It should be carefully noted, however, that Tillich is not suggesting a self-help approach to anxiety. It is common today to talk about social and existential anxieties about death, morality, and the future. But these conversations are often framed in terms of personalistic solutions, that is, salvation by works. To combat anxiety, it is said you must have a better routine, spend less time on your phone, meditate more, exercise, and eat well, etc. But Tillich is clear that these solutions are not enough. They cannot overcome the threat of nonbeing adequately. Only God is the power that overcomes nonbeing and gives us the courage to be. Accordingly, Tillich has an implicit critique of all our false, works-based solutions to anxiety, such as those we see today or others that were common during his time. We cannot save ourselves with self-help techniques or the latest methods of wholeness and healing; only the transcendent ground of divine grace provides the courage to be.

Toward the end of the book, this theological insight is more explicit. Tillich argues, "The ultimate source of the courage to be is the 'God above God'..."[25] This is what ultimately connects the courage to be with Tillich's doctrine of God. Tillich is describing God as the "God above God" in order to contrast God with the objectifications of God, that is, the domesticated God whom we might possess like an object. The true God is *beyond* theism and atheism. There is a profound logic of the cross at play here. On the cross, Jesus Christ cried out to the God who remained his God even while God abandoned him in "the darkness of doubt and meaninglessness."[26] This is the "God above God," or the God who appears on the other side of doubt, the God beyond theism and

---

24. Ibid.
25. Ibid., 186.
26. Ibid., 188.

atheism. And this God is the source of the courage to be. "The courage to be is rooted in the God who appears when God has disappeared in the anxiety of doubt."[27] The God above God is the ground and power of being, who truly meets us in the midst of our anxieties because Christ has taken up the threat of nonbeing and overcame it. That is the source of our courage to be, to accept acceptance despite unacceptability.

The Irish novelist and playwright Samuel Beckett concluded his great trilogy of novels like this: "I can't go on, I'll go on."[28] The courage to go on despite being unable to is a poetic description of Tillich's message in *The Courage to Be,* but in contrast with Beckett, Tillich does not locate this courage in the self but in the transcendent ground and power of being-itself, that is, God. Thus, he might wish to add: "I can't go on, I'll go on… *by grace.*"

---

27. Ibid., 190; italics removed.
28. I discuss Beckett and Tillich in chapter four of my book, *Christ's Wait for Godot: A Theological Appreciation of Samuel Beckett* (Columbus: Beloved Publishing, 2021). Beckett's quote is from the final page of *The Unnamable.*

3. Christ and Existence

Summary: Jesus is the Christ who manifests and establishes the New Being. This claim is central to Tillich's theology as it articulates what is, for him, the basic Christian message. Tillich's concept of New Being is not *another* being but the *fulfillment* of finite being through the reunion of estranged existence with essential being. Christ is the one who brings about salvation, which is best categorized as *healing*, not overcoming our humanity. Tillich further emphasizes the healing quality of salvation through his concept of "universal essentialization."

In Tillich's own words:

> Historically and systematically, everything else in Christianity is a corroboration of the simple assertion that Jesus is the Christ.[1]

> There is one answer which underlies all parts of the present system and which is the basic content of the Christian faith, and that is that Jesus is the Christ, the bringer of the New Being.[2]

---

1. Paul Tillich, ST2, 92.
2. Paul Tillich, ST3, 174.

The Incarnation is the manifestation of original and essential Godmanhood within and under the conditions of existence.[3]

SECONDARY QUOTES:

Tillich's is a *christomorphic* theology.... To be sure, the whole, from the beginning to end, is set within philosophical/ontological categories; nevertheless, knowledge of God and *all* theological symbolism, as Tillich repeatedly insists, come through revelation, and so, for the Christian community and theologian, through the decisive revelatory appearance of the New Being in Jesus who is the Christ.[4]

— LANGDON GILKEY

[Tillich's] central Christological claim is that as the Messiah, Jesus as the Christ ushers in a new eon that overcomes the estranged world ruled by structures of evil, structures which, according to prophetic and apocalyptic descriptions, are symbolized as demonic powers and rule individuals, nations, and even nature, producing anxiety in its forms.... Tillich contends that Christ overcomes these powers, and the sin and evil they engender, by taking on the destructive consequences of estrangement upon himself, fully maintaining his unity with God even as he sacrifices everything he could have had for himself from this unity.[5]

— LOIS MALCOLM

INTRODUCTION

The heart and norm of Paul Tillich's thought is that Jesus is the Christ who manifests and establishes the New Being. That is not always spelled out directly, but it is the central message of his theology and perhaps of all his work, whether he's talking about courage, philosophy, or faith. Tillich

---

3. Paul Tillich, *The Ground of Being*, ed. Robert M. Price (Mindvendor, 2015), 190-1.
4. Langdon Gilkey, *Gilkey on Tillich* (New York: Crossroad, 1990), 144.
5. Lois Malcolm, "Mystical and Prophetic" in *Bulletin of the North American Paul Tillich Society*, 32-4 (Fall 2006), 12.

calls it the "material norm" of theology (ST1, 50). It summarizes the basic Christian message, and is therefore, the "answer [that] is given to the question implied in our present situation and in every human situation" (ST1, 49). The New Being overcomes "the self-estrangement of our existence" (ST1, 49), which is manifested in Jesus the Christ. That Jesus the Christ manifests New Being is the object of our ultimate concern as Christians. "This norm," continues Tillich, "is the criterion for the use of all the sources of systematic theology" (ST1, 50). It is foundational, normative, and presupposed everywhere because the New Being is our ultimate concern.

This chapter will focus on answering what Tillich means by the New Being manifested in Jesus the Christ, why he uses this precise terminology, and what the overall shape of his soteriology (theory of salvation) looks like. But it is important to emphasize that the New Being manifested in Jesus the Christ is *the* central claim in Tillich's theology. A charitable reading of his thought requires us to take this claim seriously and base our reading on it before engaging in any sort of critique.

To fully understand this crucial point, I will follow volume two of his *Systematic Theology*, which begins with existence before moving to the reality of Christ. So we will first explore Tillich's doctrine of the fall and how it relates to existence, where only then can we arrive at an accurate description of his concept of the New Being in Jesus the Christ.

The fall

The fall is "a symbol for the human situation universally, not… the story of an event that happened 'once upon a time'" (ST2, 29). Tillich's preferred terminology for the fall is the "transition from essence to existence" (ST2, 29). This approach retains the temporal element implied in the symbol of the fall without requiring it to be a strictly historical event. The symbol remains temporal because Tillich insists that sin is not created by God, which means the fall cannot be *completely* demythologized. So there is still room for speaking of the fall in terms of a temporal transition or even as a story, but it is ultimately a symbol used to express a universal situation. This approach liberates theology from speculating about a specific point in creation history when human beings fell from a state of perfection; instead, the fall symbolically indicates the universal situation of all creation in the transition from essence to existence. As we will see, this effectively leads Tillich to unite creation and the fall as one and the same event.

Tillich's language about the fall as the transition from essence to existence explains and contextualizes his famous comment that existentialism is "the good luck of Christian theology. It has helped to rediscover the classical Christian interpretation of human existence" (ST2, 27). I have already noted how Tillich is not properly thought of as an *existentialist* theologian, even while he *does* think existentialism is a vital tool for the modern theologian. Thus, existentialism is "a natural ally of Christianity" (ST2, 27). He uses existentialist language about human estrangement to describe the symbol of the fall and what it means for the human situation of sin. But it is important to be clear about this distinction. Existentialism is an *ally* and *tool* for Tillich; he has not made theology into a handmaiden of existentialism.

But why is there a fall in the first place? It is necessary because of our *finite* freedom as human beings. We do not possess *ultimate* freedom. We are only free in an analogous way to divine freedom. Finite freedom operates "within the frame of a universal destiny" (ST2, 31). What Tillich means is that, in contrast to God's ultimate freedom, wherein God is God's own destiny, human finite freedom is *limited* by each person's destiny, namely, by finitude and death. God transcends the limits of freedom and destiny, but human finitude is bound to this limit. Therefore, the fall is necessary because human beings are created in the image of God with both freedom and destiny. Thus, the transition from essence to existence is universal and cosmic. He writes, "There is no individual Fall" (ST2, 32). It is not merely the fall of an individual person named Adam or Eve; the symbol of the fall involves all creation cosmically.

That explains why Tillich challenges the notion of a pre-fallen humanity, whether it is through an assumed "innocence" or the orthodox doctrine of "original perfection." Tillich calls this an absurdity that "makes the Fall completely unintelligible" (ST2, 34). How so? It is because only God is perfect by transcending both essence and existence. To *exist* means to be aware of finitude, which produces anxiety. The idea of an ideal state of being prior to the fall is problematic in that it makes unintelligible the transition from essence to existence, which is identical with the act of creation itself. It is "the original fact" (ST2, 36). What Tillich is suggesting is that "the transition from essence to existence is a universal quality of finite being. It is not an event of the past; for it ontologically precedes everything that happens in time and space" (ST2, 36).

This means that finite, created reality *is* the transition from essence to existence. To exist *is* to live in a fallen state. Every day we "fall" and miss the mark of true essence through finite existence. This effectively combines the doctrine of the fall with creation. Reinhold Niebuhr criticized Tillich for collapsing creation and the fall, and there is some element of truth that Tillich admits (ST2, 44). But he nonetheless argues, "Creation is good in its essential character. If actualized, it falls into universal estrangement through freedom and destiny" (ST2, 44). Therefore, creation and the fall do coincide to such an extent that Tillich suggests, "[T]here is no point in time and space in which created goodness was actualized and had existence" (ST2, 44). There can be no utopia of the past. The actualization of creation's essential goodness *is* the transition from essence to existence, and there is no unactualized creation. Therefore, creation and fall coincide, even though Tillich still retains the important claim that creation in *essence* is good despite the limitations of existence.

This point gets into some difficult and problematic areas of speculation, and for that reason, Tillich is purposefully brief. There is certainly room to criticize his approach, but Tillich argues it is a necessary consequence of rejecting a literal interpretation of the fall. There are two points worth noting about this before moving into less murky waters.

First, the fall highlights the "tragic-universal character of existence" (ST2, 38). What Tillich means is that "the very constitution of existence implies the transition from essence to existence" (ST2, 38). Therefore, existence is tragic. The act of freedom that leads to existential estrangement is "imbedded... In the universal destiny of existence" (ST2, 38). The doctrine of the fall is typically thought in terms of something that happened once upon a time, but Tillich's point (which is helpful to recognize) is that the transition from essence to existence is an event that takes place daily—it is the tragic fact of existence that we are not what we should be in essence. That is the basic existentialist claim, that we are estranged from our essence. Tillich will continue this line of thought into his doctrine of sin.

A second point that I have found helpful in making sense of Tillich's argument is to think of it in terms of Plato's theory of the forms.⁶ This theory in itself is a difficult one, but it may be helpful here. Plato's theory looked at the existence of beauty, goodness, and truth and asked what was the underlying power, source, or ideal that defines and unites all that is beautiful, good, and true. He concluded that there must be an essential *form* of beauty, goodness, and truth that is then actualized in the existence of things sharing these qualities. The essence of a thing is then the criteria that judges its various expressions. Similarly, defining the fall as the transition from essence to existence can affirm both the goodness of creation in essence, but it also explains the estrangement of existence from that essence. That is how Tillich unites creation and fall, and it is a major aspect of how he describes the immediacy of the fall (as opposed to it being a purely historical event in the past). All creation is estranged from its essence by the actualization of essence in existence.

For our purposes, what is significant about Tillich's doctrine of the fall is how it fits into an important pattern at the center of his theology: union-estrangement-reunion. By considering the fall as a transition from essence to existence, Tillich is suggesting that the estrangement of existence is possible because of a more original *union* between the human and divine. In other words, estrangement is not possible without first asserting a unity.

We are not estranged from God in the sense of being *strangers*, with no connection to God. Rather, we are *estranged*, which implies that we belong essentially to that which we are estranged from, namely, God. This pattern is central for Tillich's theology, but it is essential to acknowledge in his christology, where Jesus the Christ manifests the reunion of the estranged in the New Being.

Estrangement

Tillich's doctrine of sin centers around this notion of estrangement. He writes, "The state of existence is the state of estrangement. Man is estranged from the ground of his being, from other beings, and from himself" (ST2, 44). But how does estrangement relate to the biblical

---

6. This connection was first pointed out to me through David W. Musser and Joseph L. Price's book *Tillich* (Nashville: Abingdon Press, 2010), 27-31.

concept of sin? Tillich does not think "estrangement" can *replace* sin because sin involves "the personal act of turning away from that to which one belongs" (ST2, 46). However, "estrangement" is an important tool for reinterpreting the doctrine of sin. Tillich proceeds to explore estrangement and sin according to three classic concepts: *unbelief, hubris,* and *concupiscence,* which will help further illuminate his doctrine of sin.

Sin as unbelief does not mean, for Tillich, that someone questions or denies a set dogma or creed. "Unbelief" is more properly "un-faith," which involves a deeper existential denial of meaning. Unbelief consists of a turning away from one's ultimate concern, from God. Tillich thinks this is the meaning of unbelief historically. But Tillich emphasizes the existential element of unbelief because the term has been misunderstood, like faith, as intellectual agreement with an opinion, rather than an existential state of being grasped by an ultimate concern. Because God is the ground, power, and center of being, for the human to turn away from this center is to be estranged from their essential reality. Sin as unbelief is this turning away.

Sin as hubris is less problematic but still needs careful qualifications. Tillich defines this term as the "self-elevation of man into the sphere of the divine" (ST2, 50). It is the drive to become the center of one's life and the world. Tillich does not think "pride" is entirely correct as a translation of hubris because pride adds a moral quality. Hubris, however, is "universally human," as opposed to being a particular quality of human morality. Hubris can be present in both humility and pride. Hubris is thus the other side of unbelief and turning from God because it involves turning towards the self as the center of one's life, making oneself ultimate. Someone can be just as hubristic through a self-centered form of false humility as they can be in their pride. Sin as hubris is the turning toward the self.

Concupiscence is no longer a word we commonly use, but it describes a drive for complete control and power, which is produced by unbelief and hubris. The human is estranged because they are removed from their center in God and have made themselves their own center. The question is, why does the human being make this second step, striving to make themselves their own center? Concupiscence is the answer: it is rooted in the drive to become all in all, to overcome the limitations of finitude. Thus, concupiscence describes the insatiable desire to "draw the whole of reality into one's self" (ST2, 52). It is typically linked with sexual desire, but Tillich expands the concept to include all forms of insatiable want. For this, Tillich refers to Nietzsche's "will to power" and Freud's "libido." Both describe the "symptoms of concupiscence" as "the unlimited character of the strivings for knowledge, sex, and power" (ST2, 53). But neither of these describes what concupiscence is, only its expression.

With these classic categories defined, Tillich further notes that sin is both an act and a fact (ST2, 56). That means the human is responsible for personal sin and experiences guilt as a result, but sin is first universal before it is individual. Tillich frequently reminds his readers that the Apostle Paul only wrote about "sin" (singular), not "sins" (plural). Sin is a state of being.

What about evil? Especially given Tillich's concept of the fall, how are we to think about God's involvement in sin and evil? Tillich argues that God permits sin because it would be a denial of human freedom not to, which is effectively a denial of the same freedom that is the image of God in humanity. Because God cannot deny Godself, God cannot also deny the image of God in the human, including our finite freedom. Evil, then, is a self-destructive consequence of sin. It is indirectly, but not directly, willed by God through the choice to create human beings with freedom. The Bible describes God's "punishment" of sin, but Tillich insists on interpreting this symbolically. "God punishes sin by throwing the sinner into more sin.... Sin is evil because of its self-destructive consequences" (ST2, 61). Sin is its own punishment.

We might suggest that the way Tillich unites creation and fall illuminates the discussion of evil in helpful ways. The reality of sin is necessary for the actualization of essence in existence. The only way to avoid evil as the consequence of estrangement from essential being is not to exist. But God wills creation and freedom. Therefore, evil is a structural necessity as a self-destructive consequence of sin.

Tillich thinks this approach is consistent with the Christian doctrine of sin and the fall. It suggests that God does not arbitrarily send evil or suffering to people to punish them individually. A hurricane (natural evil) did not kill hundreds because God willed their punishment. Rather, universal sin (singular) led to evil as its consequence. God willed *freedom* for human beings, but the consequence was sin and evil. Moral evils such as murder and social injustice are also accounted for in the individual acts of unbelief, hubris, and especially, concupiscence. These are necessary for the *imago dei*, which is expressed in a finite freedom that mirrors God's ultimate freedom. But Tillich's broader point is that sin and evil were unavoidable. We cannot speculate about a utopian version of creation where evil might not have been a consequence of the fall; instead, creation is the actualization of essence, which necessitates estrangement from essential being by existing in freedom.

THE QUEST FOR NEW BEING

All of these points lead us to an important question: Is it possible to overcome our estrangement? Humanly, it is impossible. "'Then who can be saved?' ... '[F]or mortals it is impossible, but for God all things are possible'" (Mt. 19:24-5, NRSV). If existence is itself this state of estrangement, then this state of being raises a question that can only be answered by *New Being*.

Before moving to Tillich's soteriology as the answer to the question of estrangement, it is important to consider his critique of any self-generated attempts at overcoming estrangement. The question of estrangement cannot be answered by ourselves. Tillich is not projecting an answer *from* the question. Indeed, the opposite is true. The question is possible *because* of the presence of grace, of the New Being that reunites the estranged.

Tillich describes this limitation classically as the "bondage of the will," which speaks to "the inability of man to break through his estrangement" (ST2, 79). Finite freedom is limited by destiny. The bondage Tillich is describing is not determinism but a result of the polarity of freedom and destiny. "Only what is essentially free," Tillich notes, "can come under existential bondage" (ST2, 79). Tillich's answer to this predicament is *divine grace,* which "does not destroy essential freedom; but it does what freedom under the conditions of existence cannot do, namely, it reunites the estranged" (ST2, 79). Salvation is reunion, but reunion is only possible by a gracious reality of New Being. It is not possible for finite being to overcome estrangement; only by grace is it possible for being-itself (for God) to reunite what was estranged. This point further articulates Tillich's central pattern: union (essence) - estrangement (existence) - reunion (New Being).

Tillich is clear that grace is not *alien* to human nature, even if we cannot generate it. Rather, grace is already paradoxically present in our situation of estrangement. Tillich writes, "The question of salvation can be asked only if salvation is already at work" (ST2, 80). Both legalism and Pelagianism are based on this reality. Because grace is already present, legalism and Pelagianism throw the individual back on their own strength to save and redeem themselves. However, Tillich stresses that "Only a New Being can produce a new action" (ST2, 80). While grace is not totally foreign to human life—or else it would not be something we could receive—the presence of preparatory grace does not mean self-salvation is possible. Instead, the presence of preparatory grace is what makes an analysis of the situation of estrangement possible. But we must recognize that we cannot, as finite creatures, overcome estrangement. The reunion of estranged being is only possible through New Being, that is, through Jesus as the Christ.

It is vital to recognize how deeply committed Tillich is to a theology of grace. The preceding analysis of estrangement is not the first or most foundational step in his argument (even if it is considered first for systematic convenience). Logically, the analysis of the situation comes first, but theologically, the most consequential reality is the New Being revealed in Jesus as the Christ; estrangement is acknowledged *because* of the presence of grace in the finite situation. Indeed, for Tillich, "even the awareness of estrangement and the desire for salvation are *effects* of the presence of saving power, in other words, of revelatory experiences" (ST2, 86; emphasis mine).

The New Being can be received because it is already at work among estranged humanity; that is what makes Tillich's analysis of the situation possible in the first place. He examines existential estrangement, not to throw the individual back upon themselves to morally perfect their lives. Nor does he move "from below" to project a doctrine of salvation. Rather, this analysis was designed to show the utter *impossibility* of self-salvation. Likewise, it shows how Tillich is not arguing that the message of Christian salvation is derived from the analysis of the situation. Instead, an awareness of the situation of estrangement is possible only by grace.

Christ and Existence

Messiah, Paradox, and Incarnation

Jesus as the Christ establishes the New Being, which overcomes finite estrangement. The New Being is the "aim of history," which occurs "in the center of history" and "gives history a center," even though Christian faith is also aware of the "not-yet" of the New Being (ST2, 87-8). Tillich avoids speaking of "Jesus Christ" and instead prefers using a fuller phrase: "Jesus who is the Christ," or "Jesus as the Christ," or more simply, "Jesus the Christ" (ST2, 98). The point is to retain the Messianic function of the title "Christ."

The Messiah symbol indicates both a historical and transhistorical meaning: "The Messiah does not save individuals in a path leading out of historical existence; he is to transform historical existence" (ST2, 88). In Judaism, the expected Messiah is the anointed King, who will establish the kingdom of peace and justice. The individualized concept of Jesus as a "personal savior" obscures this more social dimension, seen especially in the symbol of "the Kingdom of God." The New Being cannot be limited to purely individual salvation. It also excludes any concept of salvation as a means of escaping the earth. Christ is not the destruction of finite, historical being, but rather, the *fulfillment* of finitude "by conquering its estrangement" (ST2, 88). At the same time, however, there is a transhistorical reality in the symbol "Christ." It is universally valid because it unites the horizontal and vertical directions.

Tillich calls the central Christian message that Jesus is the Christ a "paradox" because it indicates a new reality established by grace. The Christian message goes against the self-understanding and expectations of human beings. It goes against "man's ordinary interpretation of his predicament with respect to himself, his world, and the ultimate underlying both of them" (ST2, 92). But "paradox is not nonsense," even though it challenges ordinary perspectives.

That is important to underline because it means the Christian message can be entirely rational even while upholding the reality of paradox, in contrast with theologies that make the Christian message into something nonsensical. Divine revelation is still central, for Tillich, because paradox means the in-breaking of a new, divine reality in both the historical and transhistorical sense. As we've seen, for Tillich, grace is not something alien to human nature. While self-salvation is impossible (or, in this context, rationally leaping up into revelation from a situation of finitude is impossible), salvation and the knowledge of the New Being are nonetheless *not* irrational or alien to human nature. In other words, the Christian message is sown among soil that is prepared to receive it. And it is prepared because the reality of grace is already present.

But what then is the paradox of Jesus as the Christ? Tillich writes, "The paradox of the Christian message is that in *one* personal life essential manhood has appeared under the conditions of existence without being conquered by them" (ST2, 94). And this appearance is a *divine* presence in Christ for that reason. God is the one who overcomes (as we saw in chapter two), and the divine in Jesus the Christ is this power to overcome the conditions of existence and manifest New Being among us. Thus, the paradox is the *incarnation*, that God is manifest in this person, Jesus of Nazareth, who is the Christ. Therefore, "It is the eternal relation of God to man which is manifest in the Christ" (ST2, 96). Jesus is the incarnate Word, but the incarnation also manifests God's general relation to human beings as such.

It is interesting that in this connection, Tillich considers the question of life on other planets. The universal relation manifested in Christ is cosmic and not limited to the earth. Tillich claims the possibility "of other divine manifestation in other areas or periods of being" (ST2, 96). This was written as the space race was beginning (Sputnik launched in 1957, the same year volume two was published), but in other works, Tillich shows an interest in this question of salvation beyond our universe and the possibility of life on other planets that might also have manifestations of the divine.[7] It is an interesting question, but it demonstrates that, for Tillich, the divine manifestation in Christ is at once particular and universal—it manifests in one person God's cosmic relation to the world. For Tillich, because of this cosmic relation, there can be no world that exists "without the operation of saving power" (ST2, 96). There is congruence between the particular manifestation of Christ and its universal significance.

---

7. See Tillich's essay, "The Effects of Space Exploration on Man's Condition and Stature" in *The Future of Religions* (New York: Harper & Row, 1966), 39-51.

Christ and Existence

Jesus as the Christ who brings New Being

The Christian message claims that Jesus is the Christ who brings the New Being. The New Being overcomes the estrangement of sin without destroying finitude; instead, it is the fulfillment of finite being. The New Being is a symbol not only of individual reunion with essential being, but it also refers to the Kingdom of God, which is the new age. Thus, both realities take on a "now" and "not yet" quality. The New Being overcomes the universal estrangement of existential being from essential being, and accordingly, Christ manifests essential being under the conditions of existence in a way that conquers the estrangement of essence and existence.

It will be helpful to work backwards from Tillich's definition of "New Being" to his complex work on Jesus as the Christ. Tillich writes:

> At this point it may be recalled that the term "being," when applied to God as an initial statement about him, was interpreted as the "power of being" or, negatively expressed, as the power to resist nonbeing. In an analogous way the term "New Being," when applied to Jesus as the Christ, points to the power in him which conquers existential estrangement. To experience the New Being in Jesus as the Christ means to experience the power in him which has conquered existential estrangement in himself and in everyone who participates in him.[8]

New Being, then, refers to the power that overcomes estrangement. It is, for Tillich, a concept that "re-establishes the meaning of grace" (ST2, 125). That is because New Being points to the divine power that is fundamentally *a gift*, and not the reward of some good work. Tillich thinks it is impossible to speak meaningfully about grace without understanding being and the power of being in this way. The conditions of estrangement are overcome by the power of being, which brings New Being through Jesus as the Christ.

The quest for New Being is fulfilled in Jesus as the Christ. The "basic Christian assertion" is that "Essential God-Manhood has appeared within existence and subjected itself to the conditions of existence without being conquered by them" (ST2, 98). If we translate this into more classical

---

8. Paul Tillich, ST2, 125.

terms, what Tillich is saying is that Jesus as the Christ manifests the power of being-itself (of God) through his personal life within the conditions of sinful humanity without being overcome by those conditions; Christ overcomes the situation of estrangement and sin by participating in those conditions. Gregory of Nazianzus' incarnational framework—"The unassumed is the unhealed"—articulates something similar. The power of New Being takes part in the limitations of estrangement without being overcome by them. Christ overcomes by living a personal life in the power of the New Being. Therefore, Jesus is the Christ who brings New Being, the power to conquer estrangement and reunite essential and existential being. That which is assumed is healed.

Central to Tillich's vision of salvation is our participation in the New Being, which is effectively identical in meaning to the Pauline phrase, "in Christ." Tillich writes, "If Jesus as the Christ represents the essential unity between God and man appearing under the conditions of existential estrangement, every human being is, by this very fact, asked to take on the 'form of the Christ.' Being Christ-like means participating fully in the New Being present in him" (ST2, 122). Participation in New Being is a holistic model of salvation that avoids the transactional language sometimes used to describe grace in terms dangerously close to making it a commodity one earns through saying the sinner's prayer or having faith. The language of participation that Tillich uses shifts the focus from a transaction to the power of being that is manifest in the New Being.

Another way to think of this is to suggest that Tillich's model of salvation focuses more on Christ's saving *life* than on his death. Of course, the death of Jesus is vital, but salvation is not the result of a transaction that took place on the cross over our heads. Rather, salvation is established, the New Being is manifested, in and through Christ's *life* lived within the conditions of estrangement without being overcome by them. Christ overcomes estrangement with his life.

Paul writes in Romans 5:10, "For if while we were enemies we were reconciled to God through the death of his Son, much more surely, having been reconciled, will we be saved *by his life*" (NRSVue, emphasis mine). Separating Christ's life from his death is a mistake, for Tillich. Theories of atonement have often done exactly that, but Tillich is interested in a more holistic approach to salvation. Thus, "the suffering of Jesus as the Christ is an expression of the New Being in him" (ST2, 124). The death of Jesus is necessary to affirm that he is the Christ, but it should not be separated from the saving significance of participation in the life of Christ, which establishes New Being among us.

Because of the symbolic nature of the title "Christ," it is necessary, for Tillich, that "He who is the Christ has to die for his acceptance of the title 'Christ'" (ST2, 97). Christ's death "proves and confirms" that Jesus is the Christ (ST2, 123). Thus, the cross is not a transaction but the culmination and verification of an entire life lived in the power of New Being.

The personal life of Christ overcomes the marks of estrangement. With this approach, Tillich is striving to reinterpret what was traditionally known as the "sinlessness of Jesus." The concept of sinlessness risks denying the humanity of Jesus, who is the Christ that overcomes. It is more important, for Tillich, to stress the power that overcomes the temptations of finitude. Tillich thinks the biblical portrait of Christ is not negative but positive: it emphasizes Christ's complete finitude, the reality of his temptations, and his victory over them. Jesus as the Christ lived within the conditions of estrangement and precisely because of this fact, overcomes estrangement in his personal life by the power of being-itself.

Another way of describing this power is that Jesus the Christ lives in an "undisrupted unity of the center of his being with God" (ST2, 138). That means Jesus has defended the essential unity of God and humanity against the conditions of estrangement that constantly threaten it. Finally, it also means that Jesus the Christ lives out "the self-surrendering love which represents and actualizes the divine love in taking the existential self-destruction upon himself" (ST2, 138). The substance of Christ as the manifestation of New Being is untouched, even if it is genuinely threatened and attacked by the conditions of estrangement. A Christ who never experiences the threats of estrangement would not be capable of manifesting the power of New Being that overcomes them through the personal life of Jesus the Christ, nor would participation in this New Being lead to the healing salvation that is proclaimed in this symbol.

This approach is a holistic vision of salvation, one that is closer to the notion that salvation is *healing* and not a transactional form of redemption. Tillich emphasizes this directly:

> With respect to both the original meaning of salvation (from *salvus,* "healed") and our present situation, it may be adequate to interpret salva-

tion as "healing." ... [H]ealing means reuniting that which is estranged, giving a center to what is split, overcoming the split between God and man, man and his world, man and himself. Out of this interpretation of salvation, the concept of the New Being has grown. Salvation is reclaiming from the old and transferring into the New Being.... If Christianity derives salvation from the appearance of Jesus as the Christ, it does not separate salvation through the Christ from the processes of salvation, that is, of healing, which occur throughout all history.[9]

Thinking about salvation in terms of "healing" is a helpful shift that Tillich proposes with his concept of the New Being. In a sidebar to this chapter, this healing motif will be explored more directly in relation to the Western atonement theories, especially one known as penal substitution, which has problematic connotations that Tillich directly rejects.

For Tillich, the New Being re-establishes the unity between God and humanity. Thus, it is a healing and reconciling work that has been accomplished through the personal life of Jesus as the Christ, who manifests the New Being and overcomes estrangement from within its conditions. The paradox of Christ, which is the paradox of incarnation, is thus connected with the paradox of salvation itself because salvation *is* participation in the New Being of Jesus as the Christ. Jesus saves human beings from the old being of existential estrangement and its self-destructive consequences, yet that saving work is paradoxical in that the individual remains simultaneously justified and sinful. Tillich writes, "The christological paradox and the paradox of the justification of the sinner are one and the same paradox" (ST2, 150). What is the content of this paradox? In short, "It is the paradox of God accepting a world which rejects him" (ST2, 150).

THREEFOLD CHARACTER OF SALVATION

Tillich concludes volume two by considering the threefold character of salvation, which includes 1) participation in the New Being (regeneration), 2) acceptance of the New Being (justification), and 3) transformation by the New Being (sanctification).

Tillich considers in this volume (ST2) the "objective" side of salva-

---

9. Paul Tillich, ST2, 166

tion, while volume three considers the "subjective" side within the category of "Spiritual Presence." The reality of the New Being precedes any subjective participation in it. Tillich cites the "Protestant Principle—that in relation to God everything is done by God" (ST3, 135). Salvation is first God's work, which is important to stress because these categories can be misunderstood as works necessary for salvation. But that is not Tillich's claim. Instead, the threefold character of salvation describes the objective work of Jesus as the Christ who brings the New Being.

1) Participation in the New Being relates to regeneration and is akin to the "new birth," or "the state of having been drawn into the new reality manifest in Jesus as the Christ" (ST2, 177). The power of the New Being lays hold of the individual in bondage to the old being and brings about a new state of being. It is a power that calls the individual to turn away from the old way by breaking through the estrangement of existence by grace.

2) Acceptance of the New Being relates to justification, which "brings the element of 'in spite of' into the process of salvation" (ST2, 178). The "in spite of" is an important element here, which we discussed in the sidebar on *The Courage to Be*. Justification does not deny the reality of sin or estrangement, which are the conditions of finitude, nor does it overlook doubt and anxiety. Rather, it is the courage to accept acceptance in spite of being unacceptable. This is the paradox of *simul peccator, simul justus*—that we are once justified and sinful. This element of "in spite of" is, for Tillich, "decisive for the whole Christian message as the salvation from despair about one's guilt" (ST2, 178). It is by grace alone that this acceptance is given; "there is nothing in man which enables God to accept him" (ST2, 179). But it is necessary to accept this acceptance.

For Tillich, "justification by faith" is an incomplete and dangerous distortion of what the Bible teaches because it implies that faith is a work that *produces* justification. Instead, he is emphatic about using the full phrase, "justification by grace through faith." That is because the cause of justification is not faith but God's grace. The faith that accepts acceptance is "the channel through which grace is mediated to man" (ST2, 179).

3) Transformation by the New Being relates to sanctification. The first two categories describe the reunion of what is estranged—"Regeneration as the actual reunion, Justification as the paradoxical character of this reunion, both as accepting the unacceptable" (ST2, 179). This third cate-

gory describes the process that follows the event of reunion. Tillich explains, "Sanctification is the process in which the power of the New Being transforms personality and community, inside and outside the church" (ST2, 179-80). That points ahead to volume three, which describes the subjective element in this threefold character of salvation.

Because it is so closely related to the New Being, I want to consider this subjective aspect briefly. Tillich describes the subjective character of New Being in volume three as "receptive," "paradoxical," and "anticipatory" (ST3, 133). These correspond to the three categories outlined above. Regeneration is, subjectively, the passive reception by the Spirit of regeneration. Justification is the *courage* to be in spite of nonbeing through the Spirit. Sanctification is *hope* for the fulfillment of salvation. This is not an order that follows one after the other; instead, these are "present wherever faith occurs" (ST3, 133). Tillich summarizes this subjective aspect:

> [F]aith has three elements: first, the element of being opened up by the Spiritual Presence; second, the element of accepting it in spite of the infinite gap between the divine Spirit and the human spirit; and third, the element of expecting final participation in the transcendent unity of unambiguous life.[10]

An interesting aspect of this subjective realization is how Tillich breaks down the classic distinctions between who is "in" and "out." He rejects the claim that participation in the New Being is exclusively located within the Christian church. That relates to his critique of the sacred-secular divide, which we discussed in chapter one. Thus, Tillich affirms that "there is always New Being in history.... But this participation is fragmentary" (ST3, 140). This fragmentary character indicates the eschatological dimension of theology, which looks ahead to the fulfillment of reunion in the eschaton (new creation). This claim that the reality of New Being is always present in history relates to a final point we will discuss: Tillich's argument for universalism.

---

10. Paul Tillich, ST3, 133.

Universal Essentialization

Tillich makes a strong case for the universal restoration of all things (which he calls "universal essentialization"), and in many ways, it is an essential presupposition of and conclusion to his theology. This approach also clarifies the meaning of salvation for Tillich. He addresses it directly in volumes two and three.

In volume two, he argues against particularism (that only some will be saved). He calls this view "unbiblical but nevertheless ecclesiastical," meaning it is widely accepted in the church despite its lack of support from the Bible. He defines particularism as "the belief that salvation is either total or non-existent" (ST2, 167). In other words, it is the belief that some will be saved and others will be damned, that salvation is either total for some or non-existent for others. This approach treats salvation like a commodity or an object, rather than as a healing event of New Being. Thus, particularism is a black-and-white approach to healing, which Tillich finds unhelpful and unbiblical. It is a common belief, but Tillich calls it an "absurd and demonic idea" (ST2, 167). Theologies of universalism have tried to escape particularism. However, Tillich thinks universalist theologies are rarely successful because the dichotomy of saved/unsaved is still presupposed in their approach.

Tillich identifies the root of this particularist dichotomy in a faulty view of salvation as a *transaction,* rather than salvation as *healing.* He explains:

> Only if salvation is understood as healing and saving power through the New Being in all history is the problem put on another level. In some degree all men participate in the healing power of the New Being. Otherwise, they would have no being. The self-destructive consequences of estrangement would have destroyed them. But no men are totally healed, not even those who have encountered the healing power as it appears in Jesus as the Christ.[11]

By viewing salvation as a matter of being "in" or "out," particularism has misunderstood salvation itself and thus spawned the idea of a dualistic

---

11. Paul Tillich, ST2, 167.

afterlife in which a lucky few are saved and the majority are condemned. Universalism also makes this error by retaining the either-or framework, even though it argues for the total salvation of all. Tillich is proposing, in contrast, a "healing" view of salvation, which offers a more nuanced framework. Because *no one* is fully healed here and now, *but also* because no one is *without* the power of the New Being (or else they would not exist), then the harsh question of who is "in" and "out" makes little sense. *Everyone* is both in and out at the same time, partially healed but not totally. It is important to remember that healing salvation means reunion with essential being, which is never fully possible under the conditions of finitude. Thus, there is always a now and not-yet quality to salvation.

No one has arrived at full healing, yet the New Being has abandoned no one, and therefore, the basic logic behind particularism—which separates people into the black-and-white category of saved or unsaved—is negated. The basic problem is with particularism's faulty concept of salvation. Tillich aims for a more holistic concept of salvation as healing, where there is both a "now" and "not yet" quality to healing for all people. Thus, *no one* is totally "in" or totally "out."

This approach may raise concerns about the specific role Jesus plays in salvation. What does it mean to confess that salvation is in Jesus as the Christ? Tillich writes, "The answer cannot be that there is no saving power apart from him but that he is the ultimate criterion of every healing and saving process" (ST2, 167-8). It is important to think through this statement with the concept of salvation as healing in mind, not salvation as a transaction. Tillich is saying that all healing processes involve participation in the New Being, but that does not mean there are no healing processes apart from Jesus (that is, apart from Christianity). That opens up the door for religious pluralism, even though Tillich thinks Jesus is the *ultimate criterion* for every healing process. "Therefore," Tillich explains, "wherever there is saving power in mankind, it must be judged by the saving power in Jesus as the Christ" (ST2, 168). This move points ahead to the eschatological dimension, which Tillich most fully explores in volume three.

In the final sections of volume three, Tillich considers the Kingdom of God within history and then as "the end of history or eternal life." Here he returns to the question of universalism. He comments how the concept of "twofold eternal destiny contradicts the idea of God's permanent creation of the finite as something 'very good'" (ST3, 407-8). For something to "be" means it participates in the ground and power of being, that is, God, and thus, it exists through divine love. The dualism of heaven/hell is inconsistent with the fact that God transcends and grounds being as being-itself. Therefore, the heaven/hell dichotomy is contradicted by the nature of God as creator.

Particularism also goes against human nature because no person is fully healed or fully unhealed. That point was already raised but Tillich makes this critique sharper, writing, "The doctrine of the ambiguity of all human goodness and of the dependence of salvation on the divine grace alone either leads us back to the doctrine of double predestination or leads us forward to the doctrine of universal essentialization" (ST3, 408). Universal essentialization is Tillich's term for the reunion of estrange being, which entails healing and salvation. Tillich argues further that individual freedom and destiny is united "in such a way that it is as impossible to separate one from the other as it is, consequently, to separate the eternal destiny of any individual from the destiny of the whole race and of being in all its manifestations" (ST3, 408-9). In other words, the fate of humanity is irrevocably linked.

The logic of particularism is rooted in a false individualism that ignores the reality that no individual is complete without the social conditions that lead to their existence. "No man is an island." That leads to a powerful conclusion: "Whoever condemns anyone to eternal death condemns himself, because his essence and that of the other cannot be absolutely separated" (ST3, 409). The division of persons into saved and unsaved is an act of violence against the self that cannot be maintained in light of the realities of the human community and its profound interconnectivity. In other words, humanity cannot be so neatly divided without doing damage to its interconnected realities.

So Tillich's argument against particularism is twofold: First, it contradicts the nature of God, and second, it contradicts the nature of humanity. Double predestination is the only alternative to this situation, but Tillich finds that this introduces a demonic split in the being of God, which is unacceptable and perhaps makes the issue worse.

However, Tillich is also sympathetic about the *reasons* why the church historically rejected universalism. He comments in reference to Origen that the reason the church rejected the *apokatastasis* (universal restoration) is that this "expectation seemed to remove the seriousness implied in such absolute threats and hopes as 'being lost' or 'being saved'" (ST3, 407). However, within Tillich's more holistic framework of healing, the transactional aspect of particularism is removed, yet the seriousness of existential loss remains. Therefore, the seriousness does not involve the loss of salvation but rather the danger of wasting "one's potentialities" (ST3, 407). Thus, the term "essentialization" is preferred because it joins the despair of this loss with the assurance of elevating "the positive within existence (even in the most unfulfilled life) into eternity" (ST3, 407). Remember that for Tillich, no one is fully healed or unhealed, and therefore, all will be elevated to eternity regardless of the degree of fulfilled potential or unfulfilled.

To fully grasp what this means, we need to step back and consider what Tillich means by eternal life, although we will consider this more fully in the next chapter. For Tillich, the idea of an immortal soul is unchristian. The Christian faith confesses a bodily resurrection to eternal life. But what is eternal life? It is participation in the divine life, where every finite event in human history is elevated into eternity. The "positive content" of history is retained, but life is liberated from the negative element. The negative element is that which results from existential estrangement. Tillich explains, "Eternal Life, then, includes the positive content of history, liberated from its negative distortions and fulfilled in its potentialities" (ST3, 397). That means, whatever happens in human history "contributes in every moment of time to the Kingdom of God and its eternal life" (ST3, 398).

Eternity, in this sense, is not an endless future but rather the "end of history" and thus the end of time. Time is, for Tillich, a condition of finitude reflecting our estrangement from essential being. Essentialization will therefore include the transcendence of time. But because eternity is not somewhere in the future but that which transcends finitude, the eternal is present in every moment. That fact "gives the eschatological symbol its urgency and seriousness" (ST3, 396).

Eternal life is participation in the life of the God who overcomes. Tillich writes, "The Divine Life is the eternal conquest of the negative; this is its blessedness" (ST3, 405). Accordingly, the final judgment is not a mythological trial of individual human beings for all the right or wrong they have done. Instead, it is a cosmic display of God's triumph over evil.

Tillich uses the biblical metaphor of God as a "burning fire" to explain this point. Nothing positive is consumed or lost in the fires of divine judgment. Rather, God re-affirms the goodness of creation, which is grounded in God's own goodness. If anything good were to be lost or annihilated (such as a creature made in God's image or a part of creation God called "very good"), that would mean God is not true to Godself as the ground and power of being (as creator). Thus, divine judgment means *liberation* from the negative distortions of life.

Eternal life overcomes finitude; the New Being is reunited life that participates in the Divine Life. That participation is real for humanity here and now by grace, but there is always the "now" and "not yet" quality in which the fulfillment of life in Eternal Life will be complete at the end of history. We participate in New Being now in anticipation of the end of history and eternal life. Tillich's pattern of union-estrangement-reunion also bears this eschatological caveat.

All these points are helpful because they clarify the meaning of salvation for Tillich. The healing power of New Being is never completely absent or fulfilled in time for any person. However, the New Being is active for all creation here and now, with the hopeful expectation of eternal life, in which the negatives of existence will be overcome by the burning fire of God's love and all the positives of history will be elevated to the eternal.

Eternity "does not mean a continuation of temporal life after death, but it means a quality which transcends temporality" (ST3, 410). That point is difficult to grasp given the avalanche of speculation in Christian thought regarding "heaven" and "hell." The concept of an immortal soul was a Platonic idea used by some in the early church, but Tillich thinks it was used mistakenly. Worse yet, the concept of immortality replaced the biblical emphasis on resurrection. But the resurrection of the body, for Tillich, is a "highly symbolic" concept. He summarizes the meaning of this symbol as indicating "that the Kingdom of God includes all dimensions of being. The whole personality participates in Eternal Life" (ST3, 412-3). This symbol thus retains the uniqueness of each individual. Resurrection of the body means the whole self is elevated to participate in the divine life, which includes self-consciousness. So Tillich is not envisioning a cosmic return to God, wherein all persons are muddled together in an unidentifiable mass. Rather, the symbol "resurrection of the body" retains individual uniqueness. Thus, resurrection is not the beginning of a new reality but the transformation of the old.

Finally, Tillich concludes by reflecting on what universal essentialization might mean for God. There is always the danger in eschatology of making religious symbols into "products of man's wishful imagination" (ST3, 423). So Tillich wants to consider what the eschaton means for the divine life. In other words, Tillich turns to reflect the significance of creation and human history for God. The result is quite moving:

> In this view the world process means something for God. He is not a separated self-sufficient entity who, driven by a whim, creates what he wants and saves whom he wants. Rather, the eternal act of creation is driven by a love which finds fulfillment only through the other one who has the freedom to reject and to accept love. God, so to speak, drives toward the actualization and essentialization of everything that has being. For the eternal dimension of what happens in the universe is the Divine Life itself. It is the content of the divine blessedness.[12]

Throughout Tillich's system, he has consistently focused on the meaning of God for the human situation. But here, on the final pages, he considers the meaning of the human situation for God. Truly, history means something for God—God is not so detached or uninvolved as to create, condemn, or save arbitrarily. Rather, creation is the result of a divine love that is fulfilled through the essentialization of all things. In other words, the universal essentialization of all creation confirms the reality of God's love. God would not be true to Godself if anyone or anything were lost.

---

12. Paul Tillich, ST3, 422.

Sermon: You Are Accepted

"You are accepted" is arguably Tillich's most famous sermon, and for good reason. It articulates how he proclaims the gospel message that Jesus the Christ brings New Being.

Tillich preached on Romans 5:20—"where sin abounded, grace did much more abound"—a passage he thinks summarizes Paul's message. But the words "sin" and "grace," Tillich comments, are strange to us "because they are so well-known."[1] Most of Tillich's sermons were for an audience "largely outside the Christian circle…"[2] In that context, "the traditional Biblical terms would have no meaning. Therefore, I was obliged to seek a language which expresses in other terms the human experience to which the biblical and ecclesiastical terminology point."[3]

Tillich defines sin as "separation," emphasizing how *sin* (not sin*s*) indicates a state of being. Because of this definition, grace is necessary for understanding sin: "We do not even have a knowledge of sin unless we have already experienced the unity of life, which is grace."[4] But grace is also known in relation to sin as the separation of life. Both terms are diffi-

---

1. Paul Tillich, *The Shaking of the Foundations* (New York: Charles Scribner's Sons, 1948), 153.
2. Ibid., vii.
3. Ibid.
4. Ibid., 155.

cult to describe. However, Tillich defines grace in terms that should be familiar to us now:

> In grace, something is overcome; grace occurs "in spite of" something; grace occurs in spite of separation and estrangement. Grace is the *re*union of life with life, the *re*conciliation of the self with itself. Grace is the acceptance of that which is rejected. Grace transforms fate into a meaningful destiny; it changes guilt into confidence and courage. There is something triumphant in the word "grace": in spite of the abounding of sin grace abounds much more.[5]

Sin is then described as social loneliness, self-hatred, and self-estrangement, and finally, estrangement from the ground of being. The ultimate form of estrangement, which is the source of estrangement from self and other, is estrangement from God: "[W]e are estranged from the origin and aim of our life."[6] And this is a situation we cannot escape. "That fact brings us to the ultimate depth of sin: separated and yet bound, estranged and yet belonging, destroyed and yet preserved, the state which is called despair."[7] This despair is sin in its most profound sense.

The words of Paul describe this situation powerfully. Yet Paul was not motivated by a sentimental desire for resolution. Instead, Tillich writes, his words

> describe the most overwhelming and determining experience of his life. In the picture of Jesus as the Christ, which appeared to him at the moment of his greatest separation from other men, from himself and God, he found himself accepted in spite of his being rejected. And when he found that he was accepted, he was able to accept himself and to be reconciled to others.[8]

Grace met Paul in this state of despair and overwhelmed him with the message of acceptance. Tillich asks, "Do we know what it means to be

---

5. Ibid., 158.
6. Ibid., 159.
7. Ibid., 160.
8. Ibid.

struck by grace?"⁹ It does not mean believing a certain doctrine, or even that God exists. "To believe that something *is,* is almost contrary to the meaning of grace."¹⁰ Furthermore, it is not about moral behavior modifications or good works. "Moral progress may be a fruit of grace; but it is not grace itself, and it can even prevent us from receiving grace."¹¹ Tillich describes the dangers of any religion that emphasizes the need to act better or believe correctly, but does so without the grace that meets us in the situation of estrangement. Without that grace, faith and morality are empty.

Divine grace meets us not through our works of believing or doing, but freely and undeservedly in the midst of unacceptability. We strive to make ourselves acceptable through belief or good works, but it is never enough. Instead, divine grace must meet us and overwhelm us like it did Paul. It is a grace that breaks through estrangement. It speaks directly to our situation, breaking through our darkness and sin, with this message:

> "You are accepted. *You are accepted,* accepted by that which is greater than you, and the name of which you do not know.... Do not seek anything; do not perform anything; do not intend anything. *Simply accept the fact that you are accepted!*"¹²

That is the experience of grace. Nothing is required of us but simple acceptance. This message liberates and empowers us to accept ourselves, each other, and to strive to overcome the separation of life. Because we are accepted and reunited with the ground and power of being, we are given the grace to live in acceptance and accept others and ourselves, to reunite the estranged.

In this sermon, Tillich translates sin and grace into terms existentially relevant for his audience, and he describes the message of New Being, where that which was estranged is reunited with the ground and power of being. It is a reality that is "now" and "not yet," which points ahead to a universal essentialization. But here and now we live in the power of grace, through the message that we are accepted in spite of unacceptability.

---

9. Ibid., 161.
10. Ibid.
11. Ibid.
12. Ibid., 162.

Salvation

In another sermon, Tillich helpfully describes what salvation is and is not. Like sin and grace, the word "salvation" should be redefined for our situation today. Going back to the Latin root of the word, Tillich defines salvation in terms of liberation and healing. Both terms indicate that human beings live estranged and in bondage, which is closely related because the sick person is in bondage to their condition.

Notably, Tillich stressed that salvation is not "escaping from hell and being received in heaven..."[13] He also rejects the concept of an immortal soul or that eternal life is endless life, as discussed above. Tillich's concept of salvation challenges what salvation often means in popular imagination, whether in or out of the church. Salvation is about healing our estranged condition and participating in New Being brought about by Jesus the Christ. That participation is a life in the divine life, which is life eternal. The motif of liberation is also stressed as essential to the gospel. How does Christ heal and liberate?

Tillich describes the meaning of Christ as savior:

> And if we call Jesus, the Christ, our saviour, then we mean that in him we see the power which heals us by accepting us and which liberates us by showing us in his being a new being—a being in which there is reconciliation with ourselves, with our world, and with the divine Ground of our world and ourselves.[14]

Tillich also emphasizes how this vision of salvation is cosmic and universal, not limited to individual salvation.

> Who shall be saved, liberated, healed? The fourth gospel says: The world! The reunion with the eternal from which we come, from which we are separated, to which we shall return, is promised to everything that is. We are save not as individuals, but in unity with all others and with the universe. Our own liberation does not

---

13. Paul Tillich, *The Eternal Now* (New York: Charles Scribner's Sons, 1963), 114.
14. Ibid., 120-1.

leave the enslaved ones alone, our own healing is a part of the great healing of the world.[15]

Both points are noteworthy contributions to how we think about the meaning of salvation today. The motifs of healing and liberating are vital, but they have sometimes been downplayed with the message of escaping hell. The gospel is not the bad news of how a few people will escape hell while the majority of humanity will be tortured forever. Rather, it is the cosmic message of New Being through Jesus as the Christ.

The benefit of this approach is that the gospel becomes truly *good news* of great joy, not a message of what someone must do to avoid hell. Nor is it a message of individual escape, but a cosmic announcement of the coming Kingdom of God. It empowers the "courage to be" in our lives as we await the cosmic fulfillment of the New Being. This message is not a cause of further anxiety and guilt, but one of comfort for estranged human beings. The street preachers who believe their purpose is to proclaim a message of fear and guilt have produced a gospel of anxiety, but the gospel of Jesus as the Christ is one that relieves the burdens of human life, not adds to them. The gospel is truly good news, not the message of a divine threat. It is the message that God has overcome the threats of evil and meaninglessness, that God is for us and accepts us.

New Creation

Tillich is profoundly Pauline in his thinking—a claim that becomes clear when we see how central 2 Corinthians 5:17 is for his theology. In a sermon, Tillich summarized the gospel with words from this passage, explaining: "If I were asked to sum up the Christian message for our time in two words, I would say with Paul: It is the message of a 'New Creation.'"[16] Tillich offers an "exact" translation of the verse: "If anyone is in union with Christ he is a new being; the old state of things has passed away; there is a new state of things."[17] The "New Being," which, as we

---

15. Ibid., 121.
16. Paul Tillich, *The New Being* (New York: Charles Scribner's Sons, 1955), 15.
17. Ibid.

have seen, is so central to Tillich's thought, is a Pauline symbol. And it is, for Tillich, the sum of the gospel. In the same sermon, Tillich continues:

> Christianity is the message of the New Creation, the New Being, the New Reality which has appeared with the appearance of Jesus who for this reason, and just for this reason, is called the Christ. For the Christ, the Messiah, the selected and anointed one is He who brings the new state of things.[18]

How does the New Being come about? We live in the old state of things, yet, by being united to Christ, we also participate in the new creation. But what is the New Being? Tillich again follows Paul's lead: "It is neither circumcision, nor uncircumcision.... It meant that neither to be a Jew nor to be a pagan is ultimately important; that only one thing counts, namely, the union with Him in whom the New Reality is present."[19] In other words, the New Being is not a new religion. It is something universal; it transcends religion. "No religion matters—only a new state of things."[20] That also means that the Christian message is not about itself and its superiority to other religions.

Tillich criticizes how the gospel sometimes looks like a sales pitch for a better religious product. But this involves a "total misunderstanding of Christianity."[21] Instead, Paul says something different; it is not a new religion but the reality that something has happened "that matters, something that judges you and me, your religion and my religion. A New Creation has occurred, a New Being has appeared; and we are all asked to participate in it."[22] That means the goal of Christian proclamation is not to "convert" other religions to ours. Rather, the Christian religion stands under judgment as much as any other religion. The New Reality changes everything. The gospel is not a call to conversion; "We want only to show you something we have seen and to tell you something we have

---

18. Ibid.
19. Ibid., 16.
20. Ibid.
21. Ibid., 17.
22. Ibid.

heard: That in the midst of the old creation there is a New Creation, and that this New Creation is manifest in Jesus who is called the Christ."[23]

Therefore, the ultimate concern of Christians is not *Christianity*. Our ultimate concern and infinite passion is the New Creation. Tillich comments, "It is the greatness of Christianity that it can see how small it is."[24] The point is not to make religion an ultimate concern. That is a path to idolatry and the demonic. Instead, the point is to proclaim the New Being that has appeared in Jesus the Christ.

Continuing with Paul in 2 Corinthians 5, Tillich then explains the meaning of reconciliation. The message is this: "*Be* reconciled to God. Cease to be hostile to Him, for He is never hostile to you. The message of reconciliation is not that God needs to be reconciled."[25] Reconciliation is not appeasement. It is not about changing God's mind about us; it is about changing our mind about God. But that leads to a deeper problem. We often cannot be reconciled to God because we are unreconciled to ourselves. "[T]here is self-rejection, disgust, and even hatred of one's self. Be reconciled to God; that means at the same time, be reconciled to ourselves."[26]

Too often, Christianity proclaims a message of self-hatred for the sake of God. That is connected to this misguided idea that reconciliation is appeasement. It sets us on a treadmill of works, rather than liberating us by grace. We try to appease ourselves, to accept ourselves in our own strength. But Tillich is clear: we accept ourselves *in spite* of being unacceptable. That means being reconciled to God involves the grace to accept ourselves and live in the reconciliation accomplished in Christ. The New Creation is not the negation of the old creation. Rather, it is the "renewal of the Old…"[27] Tillich writes, "Salvation does not destroy creation; but it transforms the Old Creation into a New one."[28] Our lives are not negated and rejected in the grace of New Creation. Self-hatred is not a Christian virtue; instead, Tillich makes a compelling argument that self-hatred is precisely what we need to be freed *from*. And when we are liberated from

---

23. Ibid., 18.
24. Ibid., 19.
25. Ibid., 20.
26. Ibid., 21.
27. Ibid., 20.
28. Ibid.

self-hatred, when we are reconciled to ourselves, then and only then are we are able to be reconciled with God and to each other.

The message of reconciliation is this: You are accepted. We cannot work ourselves into this acceptance. Rather, New Creation grasps us despite our inability to accept ourselves and each other. "When the New Reality appears, one feels united with God, the ground and meaning of one's existence.... One accepts one's self as something which is eternally important, eternally loved, eternally accepted. The disgust of one's self, the hatred of one's self has disappeared."[29] That is the meaning of the gospel. Accept that you are accepted and *be* reconciled to the God who never stopped loving you, despite estrangement, sin, and self-hatred. You might have rejected yourself, given up on yourself, and even hated yourself. But God never did. Therefore, *be* reconciled—to God, to self, and to neighbor.

---

29. Ibid., 22.

Sidebar: Atonement Theories

Tillich provides an insightful framework for thinking about the various "atonement theories," while raising critical questions against a few dominant ones (particularly penal substitution). He also establishes some helpful guidelines for how to think about reconciliation in the future. He surveys three dominant theories: *Christus Victor*, the moral influence theory, and Anselm's theory of ransom (together with penal substitution), categorizing them by the dominant objective or subjective element.

The first theory, *Christus Victor* (as developed by Origen),[1] emphasizes the liberation of human beings from "the bondage of guilt and self-destruction" because of a "deal between God, Satan, and Christ in which Satan was betrayed" (ST2, 171). The theory presents a "cosmic drama" that seems to have little to do with the subjective results for human beings. It takes place "over man's head" (ST2, 171). But Tillich is careful to trace why this theory became significant for the church. The mythic dimension reflects a deeper metaphysical narrative, "the truth that the negative lives from the positive, which it distorts" (ST2, 171). The negative has no independent reality, and likewise, the demonic is a power that, as we saw in chapter one, lives off a distorted positive. The demonic is a

---

1. There is debate about this claim, but Tillich uses Origen as his example here, so I have retained his reference to Origen.

false ultimate concern, an idol. It can keep an individual in bondage and separated from God. Origen's theory thus reflects a deeper metaphysical point about how God overcomes the threats of nonbeing and finitude. Atonement is liberation from the powers of evil and death, the negative of history. But this theory needs a subjective element, which Tillich locates in "the experience of the power of the New Being in Jesus as the Christ" (ST2, 172).

The second theory is Abélard's moral influence model. The love of God displayed in Christ's death "awakens in man the answering love which is certain that, in God, love, not wrath, is the last word" (ST2, 172). Abélard's theory is entirely subjective, focusing on the effects of the cross on the individual. But that is also its downfall, since the emphasis on love without justice is a distortion. "For love becomes weakness and sentimentality if it does not include justice" (ST2, 172). It is not enough to emphasize a subjective change in the human situation without also showing an objective overcoming of the old being with the New.

The third theory is Anselm's model. Tillich thinks it became the dominant model in Western Christianity because it does "justice to [the] psychological situation" of existential estrangement and guilt. Yet it is another primarily objective model, which begins with the wrath of God against the human violations of justice. Therefore, Christ satisfies God's wrath. The weight of sin is carried by Christ and appeased. That is how this theory speaks to the psychological situation of guilt. Accordingly, the theory remains powerful because it "gives the individual the courage to accept himself in spite of his awareness that he is unacceptable" (ST2, 173). That is because Anselm's theory uncovered a "deeply hidden guilt feeling" and addressed it directly (ST2, 173).

But Tillich criticizes Anselm's model for lacking a clear subjective element. The wrath and love of God are reconciled over our heads. Furthermore, the mediator motif leads to the problematic notion that "God is the one who must be reconciled" (ST2, 169). But that does not align with the Christian message "that God, who is eternally reconciled, wants us to be reconciled to him. God reveals himself to us and reconciles us to him through the Mediator. God is always the one who acts, and the Mediator is the one through whom he acts" (ST2, 169-70). The substitutionary model reverses 2 Corinthians 5:19, "God was in Christ reconciling the world to himself." Instead, it implies that God was reconciling God's love with God's wrath, that we are saved *from God*, not *for God*.

Instead of a substitutionary model, Tillich argues that a far better model is *participation in the New Being*. This approach includes both objective and subjective elements in the atonement. Jesus the Christ brings about the New Being with his life, death, and resurrection. That unites Christ's life and work: "the being of the Christ is his work and… his work is his being" (ST2, 168). The life and work of Christ bring about the New Being, and by participating in New Being, there is reconciliation with God, neighbor, and self.

Tillich does not propose a new theory of the atonement directly, but he does establish a number of principles for the atonement. These are:

1. The atoning processes are created by God and God alone.
2. There can be no conflict between divine love and justice.
3. Divine forgiveness does not overlook or downplay sin and the depth of existential estrangement.
4. God overcomes by participating in existential estrangement and its self-destructive consequences.
5. The cross manifests God's participation in existential estrangement and its self-destructive consequences.
6. Through participation in the New Being, human beings manifest the atoning work of God by participating in the sufferings of Christ.

The first principle rejects all salvation by works, but it also emphasizes that the atonement is God's work toward the human situation of estrangement, not a work that fixes something in God. God acts to atone for human sin; Christ does not save us from God but from sin. The second principle unites the divine love and justice. The atonement does not involve a contradiction in God, but God's love and justice are united in a saving and healing act toward human estrangement. The third principle avoids a concept of forgiveness as simply overlooking a wrong. We are accepted *in spite of* being unacceptable. The "in spite of" cannot be removed.

The fourth and fifth principles introduce an important dimension regarding the atonement, one that calls back another model that was not previously considered, rooted in the thought of patristic writers such as St. Athanasius (e.g., *On the Incarnation*). This is the idea that God participates and bears the consequences of our situation of existential estrangement. Tillich separates this into God's participation and Christ's, not because these are separate but because the first grounds the second, which manifests God's participation and does not begin it. God takes the consequences of estrangement as God's own and acts to overcome them in history. The biblical passages referring to divine patience and repentance express this participation in history. Thus, Tillich can affirm that "God takes the suffering of the world upon himself" (ST2, 175). However, he is quick to add that suffering does not contradict God's eternal aseity, meaning that God's being lives of and from Godself. In other words, God does not depend on anyone or anything else to be God. God is self-sufficient. The suffering of God "is the suffering that God takes upon himself by participating in existential estrangement" (ST2, 175). In other words, God freely suffers with estranged existence, but God was not compelled to do so by anything other than God. Tillich comments, "Here the doctrine of the living God and the doctrine of the atonement coincide" (ST2, 175). God is free and living and, as such, God takes up the suffering consequences of our existential estrangement.

Christ manifests the divine participation in suffering by his death on the cross. Manifesting does not mean simply making something known. Instead, it is an "effective expression," which has "effects and consequences." The cross "is a manifestation by being actualization. It is not only actualization, but it is the central one, the criterion of all other manifestations of God's participation in the suffering of the world" (ST2, 175). The point Tillich is stressing is that the cross truly actualizes the atonement. It is not just a revelation of God's suffering, even if "The Cross is not the cause but the effective manifestation of God's taking the consequences of human guilt upon himself" (ST2, 176). The atonement is thus actualized through the cross because it involves both the subjective and objective elements.

Finally, Tillich's sixth principle stresses that because the atonement is brought about "through participation in the New Being, which is the being of Jesus as the Christ, men also participate in the manifestation of the atoning act of God. They participate in the suffering of God who takes the consequences of existential estrangement upon himself... they participate in the suffering of the Christ" (ST2, 176). This point stresses that God's suffering and its effective manifestation in the cross cannot be conceived as a substitute for human suffering. However, it does suggest that "the suffering of God, universally and in the Christ, is the power which overcomes creaturely self-destruction by participation and transformation" (ST2, 176). The aim here is to argue that substitution is not and should not be the dominant motif of the atonement. Rather, *participation* more adequately reflects the nature of God's participation in our situation and our participation in the New Being. Therefore, there is a "participation in the divine participation, accepting it and being transformed by it" (ST2, 176). That directly leads Tillich to consider the threefold character of salvation, which we previously discussed in terms of participation (regeneration), acceptance (justification), and transformation (sanctification).

With this, Tillich articulates a helpful framework for thinking about the nature of salvation and the mechanism of how it is achieved. As many today have come to challenge the dominant Western atonement models, his principles may offer fruitful avenues for approaching the doctrine of the atonement within a broader framework of salvation as the healing and liberating power of New Being.

Sidebar: Christology and the Resurrection

Tillich's christology is compelling for its effort to make the meaning of Christ existentially relevant to the human situation of anxiety and estrangement. However, many raise concerns about its orthodoxy, particularly in terms of how Tillich deals with the two natures of Jesus and the resurrection. In this sidebar, I hope to offer a charitable interpretation of these difficult and controversial issues. While Tillich's conclusions may not be palatable to all, it is important to be patient and focus on *why* Tillich argues the way he does. Often, the problems Tillich raises have been overlooked or downplayed by traditional christology. Recognizing the difficulties he uncovers is important, even if we do not follow his solutions.

Two Nature Christology

It will be helpful to begin with a vital claim from Tillich: "The christological dogma saved the church, but with very inadequate conceptual tools" (ST2, 140). In particular, Tillich has the Chalcedon formula in mind, which is the standard definition of a two nature christology. This formula, for Tillich, "saved" the church from heresies that threatened to destroy the Christian message. However, because of the limitations of that time period, they used inadequate conceptual tools. But Tillich thinks we can retain its *message* without needing to retain those inadequate tools. "Theology," he writes, "must be free from and for the concepts it uses" (ST2, 142). The conceptual *form* of a doctrine should not be confused with the *substance* indicated by it. What Tillich attempts with his christology is to update its conceptual form without losing the substance, and that point is vital to acknowledge to avoid hasty judgments of his theology.

Tillich recognizes two dangers that immediately emerge with the statement that Jesus is the Christ: a denial of either the Jesus-character or the Christ-character. Tillich remarks, "[C]hristology must always find its way on the ridge between these two chasms, and it must know that it will never completely succeed, inasmuch as it touches the divine mystery, which remains mystery even in its manifestation" (ST2, 142). Christology gets to the heart of the central Christian message, but the formulas and doctrines we have constructed are still only a grasping at something that is fundamentally a mystery. That is not a cop-out for intellectual laziness, but rather, it is a safeguard for acknowledging our limitations theologically.

The Chalcedon Formula offered one attempt to solve the dilemma, but Tillich thinks the two nature approach fails to solve it adequately. Tillich explains the problem well:

> The doctrine of the two natures in the Christ raises the right question but uses wrong conceptual tools. The basic inadequacy lies in the term "nature." When applied to man, it is ambiguous; when applied to God, it is wrong.[1]

In the nineteenth century, Friedrich Schleiermacher observed the same problem. It is inadequate to apply a fixed concept of "nature" unilaterally to both God and humanity. That would mean assuming that the nature of God and humanity is the same, but even that does not, ultimately, resolve the tension in the radical distinction between God and humanity that is said to be reconciled in Christ.

That is what Tillich means when saying that the problem identified with Chalcedon is correct, but the solution offered makes use of inadequate conceptual tools. It asks the right question, and Tillich even praises

---

1. Paul Tillich, ST2, 142.

Sidebar: Christology and the Resurrection

the "two great decisions" of the early church—Nicaea and Chalcedon—for preserving both "the Christ-character and the Jesus-character of the event of Jesus as the Christ" (ST2, 145). However, the misuse of "nature" is a central problem that cannot be overlooked. Tillich's own christology strives to retain the substance of a two-nature christology, but without its inadequacies.

A vital point Tillich makes in that direction is to recognize how the doctrine is, at its core, soteriological. The two nature doctrine is closely connected to the doctrine of salvation brought about through Jesus as the Christ. It is not just an intellectual idea. Christology is an existential concern, which either establishes our reconciliation or leaves us without hope. At stake is the entire Christian message and the promise of New Being in Christ.

Tillich rejects what is sometimes called "high" christology because of how it overemphasizes Christ's divinity, resulting in a Jesus unequal to humanity in every way. In contrast, a "low" christology is necessary, and Tillich comments that only a low christology is "truly a high christology" (ST2, 147). Furthermore, Tillich examines the ambiguity of "human nature." What is meant by this? Humanity in its essential nature, its estranged nature, or some mixture of both? It is inappropriate to exclude the ambiguities of existence, which means dropping the very concept of "human nature" in favor of "a description of the dynamics of his life" (ST2, 147).

Likewise, the concept of a divine nature is problematic. "Nature" often implies "essence," but God is beyond essence and existence. God transcends essence and should be thought of through a "more concrete expression" of essence with the notion that "God is eternally creative" (ST2, 147). So, Tillich rejects "nature" as being far too ambiguous and static to be useful for describing the mystery of Jesus as the Christ.

What is Tillich's solution? He proposes replacing the personal unity of divine and human nature in Christ with "the assertion that in Jesus as the Christ the eternal unity of God and man has become historical reality. In his being, the New Being is real, and the New Being is the re-established unity between God and man" (ST2, 148). This approach relies on the saving effects of Christ's being, rather than a static definition of two natures united in Christ. The unique and mysterious reality of Jesus as the Christ is the manifestation of the New Being, which is the reunion of estranged humanity from the ground and power of their being, that is, from God.

He aims to replace a static definition with a dynamic one. The New Being thus contains both a "now" and "not yet" reality to it, as we have seen. Thus, the dynamic quality of the New Being is a solution to the issues identified with a static, two nature definition. The arrival of Christ is the manifestation of the New Being, a dynamic and saving act of God to reunite estranged existence with Godself.

However, this solution relies on a basic point central to Tillich's theology, that there exists "an eternal unity of God and man within the divine life" (ST2, 148). Estranged being is estranged precisely because of this unity. Existence involves being alienated from essence, which is unity with the ground and power of being. Therefore, it is presupposed that there is an eternal unity between God and humanity that is broken in creation only to be reunited in the New Being. Jesus as the Christ is the manifestation in history of that reunion.

That leads Tillich to conclude that the fundamental paradox of christology is identical to "the paradox of the justification of the sinner.... It is the paradox of God accepting a world which rejects him" (ST2, 150). This point further solidifies the connection between christology and soteriology. The New Being manifested in Christ "participates in existence and conquers it" (ST2, 150). It is a dynamic ontological reality.

Most importantly, this solution reflects Tillich's existential concern. Here, christology is existentially relevant. It is not merely a question of theoretical correctness. A dogmatic repetition of traditional formulas obscures the fact that, for many, those formulas are no longer existentially important, and the only motivation for upholding them is theological orthodoxy. But if christology is a question about a person named Jesus, then the discussion revolves around a person *over there* in the past, which is a country we can only think about but cannot visit. However, if christology is about *New Being* here and now, then it is existentially relevant to our lives. Tillich's hope is that this solution moves christology closer to bearing the existential immediacy it held for the early church, who staked their lives on it.

Sidebar: Christology and the Resurrection

Resurrection

Tillich acknowledges the interdependence of the cross and resurrection as *symbols*; they are both symbol *and* reality. "In both cases something happened within existence. Otherwise the Christ would not have entered existence and could not have conquered it" (ST2, 153). However, the cross certainly took place within historical existence, but the resurrection is veiled in mystery. "The one is a highly probable fact; the other a mysterious experience of a few" (ST2, 153). That does not negate the claim that the cross and resurrection are *both* a symbol and an event, but it complicates how we understand the resurrection.

This point is crucial because it shows that Tillich does affirm that there was a real experience connected with the resurrection. It was not, in other words, purely a metaphor or a myth made up by the first disciples. There was a real event that took place to reinforce the Christ-character of Jesus and the "certainty that he who is the bringer of the new eon cannot finally have succumbed to the powers of the old eon" (ST2, 154). The New Being manifested in Christ overcame the old being. That is the foundational message of the resurrection. Christ overcomes and conquers "the destructive consequences of estrangement" (ST2, 155).

From this claim, Tillich considers three theories "which try to make the event of the Resurrection probable" (ST2, 155). The most traditional theory is the physical resurrection. Tillich considers this to be a "rationalization of the event" that interprets it according to physical categories. Therefore, it asserts that the resurrection must mean the "presence or absence of a physical body" (ST2, 155). But this rationalization leads to absurdities, such as the question about what happened to the molecules of Jesus' corpse, which Tillich thinks then compounds "into blasphemy" (ST2, 156). He dismisses this theory relatively quickly. There are only two full sentences between Tillich's description of this theory and his dismissal of it as absurd and blasphemous.

The second theory is what Tillich calls a psychological resurrection, which asserts that the resurrection was "an inner event in the minds of Jesus' adherents" (ST2, 156). Tillich thinks Paul's description of the resurrection might fit into this category. However, he rejects this theory as quickly as the physical because it denies "the reality of the event which is presupposed in the symbol" (ST2, 156). So far, Tillich has rejected the two theories common to both conservative and liberal theologies. Tillich's concept of "symbol" cuts both ways. It must involve *both* a human and divine reality. The conservative solution moves too close to supernaturalism, while the liberal solution moves too close to naturalism. Neither captures the full meaning of the resurrection symbol. So what is Tillich's solution?

Tillich describes his theory as a "restitution theory" of the resurrection. It is important to see how this tries to transcend the limitations of the previous two theories while also accepting the benefits each offers. Tillich begins by asking what the negative aspect is that the resurrection overcomes. He answers: it must overcome the disappearance of the one who manifests the New Being, including the conquest of transitoriness. A tension emerges between the transitoriness of the one who manifests the New Being and the conquest of transitoriness by New Being. From this, "something unique happened" (ST2, 157). Jesus of Nazareth is "indissolubly united" with New Being so that "wherever the New Being is present" Jesus is present. However, Jesus' presence is not "a revived (and transmuted) body, nor does it have the character of the reappearance of an individual soul" (ST2, 157). In other words, this presence is neither physical nor psychological (the first two theories). Instead, Christ's presence is that of a "spiritual presence." That means, "He 'is the Spirit' and we 'know him now' only because he is the Spirit" (ST2, 157). The result is that

> the concrete individual life of the man Jesus of Nazareth is raised above transitoriness into the eternal presence of God as Spirit. This event happened first to some of his followers… then to many others; then to Paul; then to all those who in every period experience his living presence here and now. This is the event.[2]

The experience of Christ's spiritual presence is the event connected to the resurrection symbol. It is rooted in an ecstatic confirmation that Jesus is the Christ. There is a mystical dimension to this theory that is worth noticing. The resurrection is rooted in the event of "ecstatic" confirmation, ecstatic having its root in "ecstasy," meaning an overwhelming, rapturous, and astonishing experience that displaces the self. Paul uses

---

2. Paul Tillich, ST2, 157.

Sidebar: Christology and the Resurrection

similar language in 2 Corinthians 5:13, "For if we are beside ourselves, it is for God…" (NRSVue). The verb for being "beside ourselves" is *existēmi*, which indicates a level of astonishment that is so disorienting and displacing that it can be akin to saying that someone has lost their mind. It seems that this is what Tillich is thinking of when describing the symbol of Christ's resurrection. The event is so displacing of former ways that it establishes a new position, the confirmation that Jesus is the Christ.

That is why Tillich calls it a "restitution theory." He explains, "the resurrection is the restitution of Jesus as the Christ, a restitution which is rooted in the personal unity between Jesus and God and in the impact of this unity on the minds of the apostles" (ST2, 157). This theory is closely related to the psychological theory, but has a more robust understanding of the concrete event that leads to the resurrection symbol. "[T]he experience of New Being precedes the resurrection experience" (ST2, 157-8). The restitution of Jesus as the Christ is the ecstatic experience that is tied to a resurrection event veiled in mystery.

These issues are difficult to untangle, but patient thought is rewarded. We might not accept everything Tillich suggests, but it is important to understand why he argues for this approach. Ultimately, Tillich is trying to retain the Christian substance of these doctrines while shedding any unhelpful exterior form that has become a stumbling block. We may not follow him in every aspect, but we should be patient in understanding before we are quick to judge.

4. Unambiguous Life

Summary: Life and history are ambiguous under the conditions of finitude, which leads to the quest for *unambiguous* life, Tillich's symbol for the eschatological fulfillment of being. In terms of the "now and not yet," New Being is the *now* of salvation (chapter 3), while unambiguous life is its *not yet*. Ambiguous life in the dimensions of spirit, history, and time correlates with unambiguous life, which Spiritual Presence, the Kingdom of God, and Eternal Life symbolize.

In Tillich's own words:

> Questions arising out of man's finitude are answered by the doctrine of God.... Questions arising out of man's estrangement are answered by the doctrine of Christ.... Questions arising out of the ambiguities of life are answered by the doctrine of the Spirit and its symbols.[1]

> The question of history has a final answer: the Kingdom of God.[2]

---

1. Paul Tillich, ST3, 286.
2. Paul Tillich, *The Ground of Being*, ed. Robert M. Price (Mindvendor, 2015), 76.

Secondary Quotes:

That the Spirit was important to Tillich is undoubted: his largest volume of theology is almost entirely devoted to this subject, and I know he regarded his 'doctrine of the Spirit' as not only Pauline but as the point 'where,' he once said, 'my theology is entirely biblical.'[3]

— Langdon Gilkey

The Spiritual Presence is God present to man.... The Spirit is pure grace. The experience of being grasped by the Spirit makes man whole and drives him to self-transcendence. It is an experience of healing, or salvation.[4]

— John Charles Cooper

Introduction

The third volume of Tillich's *Systematic Theology* examines life, history, eschatology, and Spirit. The volume stretches Tillich's correlation method to its limit because of the eschatological (dealing with "last things") nature of these subjects. The Christian message has a "now" and "not yet" quality about it. This tension makes volume three a unique and challenging volume. It is also the longest of the three volumes.

New Being in Christ is symbolized in the categories of life and history by "unambiguous life," which is fulfilled life, or we might say life liberated from the ambiguities of existence. A key point to recognize here is that the answer to finite ambiguities is not to escape life itself but to fulfill its potentialities. In other words, Tillich's eschatology is neither utopian nor escapist because his vision of salvation focuses on healing *this* life, not on escaping hell or going to heaven in the next life. As *healing,* salvation includes both a "now" and "not yet" dimension. Therefore, Tillich's reflections show the profound relevance of eschatology for our lives. The study

---

3. Langdon Gilkey, *Gilkey on Tillich* (New York: Crossroad, 1990), 158.
4. John Charles Cooper, *The "Spiritual Presence" in the Theology of Paul Tillich* (Macon, GA: Mercer University Press, 1997), 113.

of "last things" is often prone to empty speculation, but Tillich avoids this error by asking what eschatology means for the questions of history under the conditions of finitude.

Tillich's eschatological concern is sometimes overlooked, but it is essential to understanding his theology. In a letter to Maria Klein, written during his time as a chaplain in WWI, Tillich described himself as "an utter eschatologist..."[5] Like many others who suffered through the horrors of war, Tillich's experience with the unspeakable brutalities of death turned his mind toward the end of all things, that is, eschatology. While Tillich's early profession of being an "utter eschatologist" is more about the feeling of standing at the end of human society and his disillusionment with war, it is worth considering how deeply the question of the end of history occupied his thought.

The brutal realities of human suffering lead us to the passionate quest for unambiguous life. We all, in the face of history's evils, ask existential questions like these: "Does history have an inherent meaning and telos?" "Will the brutalities of injustice have the final word?" "Will death triumph over life?" Tillich correlates these questions with the Christian symbols of Spirit, Kingdom, and Eternity.

The quest for unambiguous life

The three symbols for unambiguous life—Spiritual Presence, Kingdom of God, and Eternal Life—express the conquest of ambiguous life in the dimensions of spirit, history, and life beyond history. Each dimension includes the other, and so the three symbols are one in substance, even if they express the same thing differently; each symbol points to the fulfillment of New Being, that is, to unambiguous life.

But first, we have to ask: What does Tillich mean by ambiguous and unambiguous life? The ambiguities of life are a result of the split between essential and existential life, which Tillich connected with the fall in volume two under the category of estrangement. The New Being manifested in Jesus as the Christ overcomes estrangement with reunion, and Tillich traces the eschatological *fulfillment* of this reunion with the symbol

---

5. Quoted in Wilhelm and Marion Pauck, *Paul Tillich: His Life & Thought*, Volume 1 (New York: Harper & Row Publishers, 1976), 51.

of unambiguous life. The basic definition of unambiguous life, then, is the "fulfillment of… [one's] essential possibilities" (ST3, 107). Therefore, ambiguous life is a life of *un*fulfilled potentialities, while unambiguous life is the fulfillment of essential potentialities.

Life under the conditions of finitude is always an ambiguous life lived *between* the potentialities of essence and its actualization in existence. We are never entirely aligned with our essential being—we are estranged—but neither are we defined solely according to our existential activities.

That is, again, why it is wrong to call Tillich an "existentialist" theologian. Existentialism commonly asserts that *we are what we do,* that existence *precedes* essence. In other words, we are thrown into life *without* an essential being, existing day by day with the radical freedom to create ourselves and define our nature. There is something remarkably freeing, yet also terrifying, about this perspective, which produces the anxiety of freedom (Kierkegaard). But that is only one side of the story, for Tillich.

In contrast, Tillich works to unite *both* existential and essential perspectives. He affirms that human beings have an essential nature created by God, but that claim puts him at odds with the existentialists, at least the most common varieties of existentialism, such as Sartre, Camus, and Kafka. For Tillich, we are *estranged* from our essential being, but our essential potentiality is not entirely lost in our estrangement. Therefore, Tillich is claiming that life develops between the *ambiguities* of essence and existence. He writes:

> Every life process has the ambiguity that the positive and negative elements are mixed in such a way that a definite separation of the negative from the positive is impossible: life at every moment is ambiguous. It is my intention to discuss the particular functions of life, not in their essential nature, separate from their existential distortion, but in the way they appear within the ambiguities of their actualization, for life is neither essential nor existential but ambiguous.[6]

These ambiguities are analyzed within the polarities of self-integration, self-creativity, and self-transcendence, which involves individualization and participation, dynamics and form, and freedom and destiny. It is

---

6. Paul Tillich, ST3, 32.

important to see how these ambiguities point toward the fulfillment of potentialities in unambiguous life. Where is unambiguous life found?

The answer to the quest for unambiguous life is received by religion; however, religion itself is *not* unambiguous life. Instead, Tillich stresses that religion is included in the ambiguities of life. That means no religion can claim it is *the* answer to the quest for unambiguous life. Unambiguous life transcends religion. This point allows Tillich to argue that—even though the Christian religion claims to have received the answer to the quest through the symbols of Spirit, Kingdom of God, and Eternal Life—this does not overcome the basic fact that our reception of every answer is *always* ambiguous. Any religion that fails to take its own ambiguity seriously will risk becoming demonic (a false ultimate) or profane (no ultimate).

A simple way to think about Tillich's concept of ambiguous life is through the cliché observation that "life is a journey." This phrase is so prevalent in our culture because it expresses something about life that we all experience. We live our lives torn between essence and existence in the ambiguous process of becoming but never fully arriving. We will never fully realize our potentialities in this life. Therefore, life is a mixture of positive and negative elements; we actualize something of our essence in life, but we also live unavoidably estranged from the fullness of our essential potentialities. Every door we choose to walk through, no matter how joyous, inevitably includes the pain of regretting the ones we didn't choose. Life is a series of closing doors.[7] Thus, what we often mean by saying that life is a journey is that we can only live authentically when we accept the ambiguities of life's process, which stands between essence and existence. Life is neither essential nor existential but ambiguous.

We often suppress this ambiguity in ourselves by presenting a perfect persona to the world. The striving to appear as if one has "arrived" is itself a symptom of life's ambiguity, but no one has or can fully actualize their being in existence. Social media is a powerful illustration of the innate human desire to present ourselves as having arrived, despite knowing well the ambiguities of our life. This tendency points to a deep longing to

---

7. This phrase is from the popular Netflix series "BoJack Horseman." Bob-Waksberg, Raphael and Peter A. Knight, writers. *BoJack Horseman,* season 1, episode 9, "Horse Majeure." Directed by Joel Moser. Netflix, August 22, 2014.

overcome ambiguous life that exists at the heart of human nature. But we cannot overcome ambiguous life apart from the divine act of grace, that is, the New Being. Our quest for unambiguous life points to an answer we cannot give ourselves, one that we can only receive freely by grace. Divine grace is again central to Tillich's thinking here. The answer to the quest for unambiguous life is received in the Christian symbols of Spiritual Presence, Kingdom of God, and Eternal Life. We will consider each of these symbols in turn.

THE SPIRITUAL PRESENCE

The first symbol of unambiguous life is "Spiritual Presence," which is Tillich's preferred term for the Spirit of God. Tillich prefers Spiritual Presence because it avoids implying that the divine Spirit is a separate being in God, but it is also because this expresses more fully what the symbol of Spirit truly indicates, namely, "the presence of the Divine life within creaturely life" (ST3, 107). This symbol correlates to the ambiguities of life in the dimension of *spirit* (lower-case). Tillich uses "spirit" for humanity and "Spirit" for God throughout ST, and this is done intentionally to show the correlation between human spirit and Spiritual Presence.

The dimension of spirit/Spirit "unites the power of being with the meaning of being" (ST3, 111). It names the "function of life which characterizes man as man and which is actualized in morality, culture, and religion" (ST3, 111). One of Tillich's central claims is that we cannot develop a doctrine of the Divine Spirit "without an understanding of spirit as a dimension of life" (ST3, 111). So it is vital to comprehend the meaning of spirit/Spirit in both the divine and human sense.

Another way to think about this use of spirit is according to the German philosophical tradition, although Tillich is not strictly bound to it. The Hegelian "spirit" (*Geist*) refers to the dialectical development of self-consciousness in history, culminating in civil society as the fulfillment of freedom. This usage involves both communal, personal, and historical elements of self-conscious life, which are integral to what it is to be human. Spirit is what makes human beings *human* in their social being, and it is what distinguishes the human community from unconscious life. Human spirit encompasses all aspects of life, indicating that it is not merely a part of life but rather the uniting power and meaning that gives life its coherence. It is crucial to see that "spirit" is here not a metaphysical idea but a social reality.

Human life in the dimension of spirit is an alienated and estranged life lived in the ambiguities of existence, but Spiritual Presence indicates wholeness and healing, a reunion with the essence of life. It is another way of describing the experience of God. But that transcendent experience correlates with the immanent experience of being "determined... by spirit as a dimension" of life (ST3, 111). The experience of (human) spirit as the unity of power and meaning "makes it possible to speak symbolically of God as Spirit of the divine Spirit" (ST3, 111). This experience of the divine Spirit in human life is often discussed through participatory metaphors such as being "in God" or "in Christ," but such metaphors need to be understood properly as symbols of the Spiritual Presence. The issue with taking such metaphors literally is that they imply a loss of human spirit. Instead, Tillich emphasizes that Spiritual Presence indicates a state of being "grasped by something ultimate and unconditional. It is still the human spirit... it goes out of itself under the impact of the divine Spirit" (ST3, 112). The biblical word for this experience is "ecstasy."

The previous sidebar on the resurrection discussed how the "ecstatic confirmation" of the resurrection is a central aspect of Tillich's "restitution theory." In that section, I connected the experience of restitution with Paul's experience of being out of himself in 2 Corinthians 5:13. Tillich's use of ecstasy in describing the experience of Spiritual Presence once again refers back to Paul's experience. It also indicates a mystical dimension to Tillich's theology of spirit/Spirit. But it is not a mysticism that *overcomes* the human spirit in the sense that we must deny ourselves and our social realities in order to participate in the divine life, but rather, Tillich's point is that this experience of God drives the human spirit *beyond* itself without *denying* its essential nature. It is *participation,* not negation. Spiritual Presence does not destroy the lived reality of human spirit, just as revelation does not destroy the rational structure of reason (ST1, part 1). Instead, the individual is grasped by the power of God, which "creates unambiguous life" (ST3, 112). It is important to note that this experience is supremely one of grace, not of works. But the argument here is vital for understanding Tillich's overall theological method. He writes:

> Man in his self-transcendence can reach for it, but man cannot grasp it, unless he is first grasped by it. Man remains himself. By the very nature of his self-transcendence, man is driven to ask the question of unambiguous life, but the answer must come to him through the creative power of the Spiritual Presence.[8]

Notice that the answer is not projected from the question. In the next chapter, I will return to this insight by arguing that Tillich's often misunderstood "method of correlation" is, in fact, deeply incarnational and rooted in the ecstatic experience of divine revelation, which answers the question of being.

In the context of this chapter, however, it is important to acknowledge Tillich's emphasis on grace because it avoids the difficulties sometimes involved in discussions of mysticism and the experience of divine Spirit, particularly the implication that we can achieve unity with the Spirit by denying our own spirit. Tillich's point is that the human spirit goes outside of itself ecstatically, *but* it does not negate itself as spirit, even when participating in the Divine Spirit. This point also underlines that unambiguous life is not a denial of this life but rather its *fulfillment*. It is the answer to the question of life's ambiguity. This answer is given by grace; we are grasped by the creative power of the divine Spirit, which creates unambiguous life. The human spirit is unable to create, grasp, or force the divine Spirit to enter the human spirit (ST3, 122).

Morality, culture, and religion, in their inherent ambiguity, represent an attempt to do precisely that, to quest after and achieve an unambiguous life by its own strength. It is a form of salvation by works, in that regard. The question of ambiguity makes all quests possible and necessary, yet the answer is not achievable within the realm of ambiguity. Unambiguous life is only and always fulfilled by grace. At the same time, morality, culture, and religion make up the structure of the human spirit, and that structure is not negated by ecstasy. This dialectic of ecstasy and structure is essential for understanding Tillich. The Spirit does not destroy the structures of spirit.

Tillich then considers the "media" of Spiritual Presence, which includes the sacraments. Tillich notes that "the Spiritual Presence cannot

---

8. Paul Tillich, ST3, 112.

be received without a sacramental element, however hidden the latter may be" (ST3, 122). Sacraments function like symbols, not signs. That means they participate in the reality they express. Or, in other words, "The Spirit 'uses' the powers of being in nature in order to 'enter' man's spirit" (ST3, 123). Tillich also considers the medium of the "word," wherein human words "become vehicles of the Spiritual Presence" and are then called "the Word of God" (ST3, 124). Tillich then goes on to explain the relationship between the Word of God and the Bible:

> The Bible does not contain words of God… but it can and in a unique way has become the "Word of God." Its uniqueness resides in the fact that it is the document of the central revelation, with respect to both its giving and its receiving sides. Every day, by its impact on people inside and outside the church, the Bible proves that it is the Spirit's most important medium in the Western tradition. But it is not the only medium, nor is everything in it always such a medium. In many of its parts it is always a potential medium, but it only becomes an actual medium to the degree that it grasps the spirit of men. No word is the Word of God unless it is the Word of God for someone…[9]

This approach is interesting because of how Tillich retains the value of the Bible without idolizing it as the only medium of the divine. Indeed, the consequence of this approach, as Tillich admits, is to accept the possibility that other words "can become the Word of God" (ST3, 125). The test is whether or not these words hit "the human mind in such a way that an ultimate concern is created" (ST3, 125). However, Tillich also suggests that the biblical witness is an ultimate criterion for judging any words that are elevated to the status of Word of God. The Bible constitutes the "ultimate touchstone for what can and cannot become the Word of God for someone. Nothing is the Word of God if it contradicts the faith and love which are the work of the Spirit and which constitute the New Being as it manifest in Jesus as the Christ" (ST3, 125). That establishes a few boundaries to protect against the danger of elevating any word to divine status, which can lead to demonic idolatry and false ultimates.

Tillich then considers the concept of an "inner" word. He emphasizes

---

9. Paul Tillich, ST3, 124-5.

that God does not speak to humanity without a medium. However, he also suggests that the Spirit is free from any particular medium. As noted above, a central claim behind these ideas is that we can understand the divine Spirit because we understand the human spirit as a dimension of life. Tillich writes, "If God were not also in man so that man could ask for God, God's speaking to man could not be perceived by man" (ST3, 127).

The question that is asked by the situation of human estrangement *can* be asked only because God is already present and at work among us. The Spirit speaks through mediums, which are human symbols that participate in the reality they indicate. God's Word comes to us through the medium of human words from the situation. Put differently, we cannot imagine an unincarnate Word, free from the limitations of the human situation. Tillich stresses that the Word is always incarnate for us, which means it comes to us through human mediums and symbols.

Tillich then considers the manifestation of Spirit in history. Here, Tillich connects Spiritual Presence with the New Being, which is situated "above the gap between essence and existence" (ST3, 138). Like the New Being, "Spiritual Presence is manifest in all history; but history as such is not the manifestation of the Spiritual Presence" (ST3, 139). Both New Being and Spiritual Presence indicate a fragmentary participation in unambiguous life, and therefore, these are eschatological symbols, even while they become manifest in history. The anticipation of this fulfillment is religion.

Tillich also returns to consider christology in this section because the Spirit was present in Jesus "without distortion" (ST3, 144). Tillich writes:

> In him the New Being appeared as the criterion of all Spiritual experiences in past and future. Though subject to individual and social conditions his human spirit was entirely grasped by the Spiritual Presence; his spirit was "possessed" by the divine Spirit or, to use another figure, "God was in him." This makes him the Christ, the decisive embodiment of the New Being for historical mankind.[10]

The blueprint for human experiences of Spiritual Presence is Jesus as the Christ, who was entirely grasped by the divine Spirit. Spiritual Pres-

---

10. Paul Tillich, ST3, 144.

ence manifests in Christ's life, and it looks like faith and love. Furthermore, a Spirit-christology implies that the Spirit makes Jesus the Christ yet this same Spirit was also at work throughout history. Jesus as the Christ "is the keystone in the arch of Spiritual manifestations in history" (ST3, 147). But Christ was "not an isolated event" (ST3, 147). Rather, the Spirit was at work in history prior to and after the appearance of Jesus, even if he is *the* keystone in the arch of that working.

Tillich then considers the manifestations of Spiritual Presence in the Spiritual Community. Tillich does not limit the Spiritual Community to the church. While he does focus on the church when analyzing the divine Spirit in ambiguity, Tillich is also interested in world religions and ideologies, such as communism. Tillich's concept of faith as a state of being grasped by an ultimate concern is, in this context, the presence of the Divine Spirit in the midst of human history. Tillich explores this in a fascinating section on religion, morality, and culture, which contains interesting comments on the nature of the Christian church in relation to these other realms.

In summary, Spiritual Presence symbolizes the presence of God in the human situation, which grasps the human spirit and lifts it up into unambiguous life by grace. Here and now, it is experienced fragmentarily as we anticipate the Kingdom of God and Eternal Life, but the Spirit is manifested in the human spirit. Tillich concludes that this manifestation bears a "healing" character, which relates this concept to his soteriology from ST2. "At this point health and salvation are identical, both being the elevation of man to the transcendent unity of the divine life" (ST3, 280). However, because this healing elevation is the healing of the human spirit, it cannot be partial. That points ahead to the symbol of the Kingdom of God, which emphasizes the social dimension of healing.

Kingdom of God

What is the meaning of history? What is its telos or goal? These questions lead to the quest for unambiguous life *in* and *beyond* history. The question of history and its ambiguities points toward an answer *beyond* history: "the aim of history does not lie in history" (ST3, 311). The two symbols that complete volume three are The Kingdom of God and Eternal Life; the former refers to unambiguous life *in* history, while the latter refers to unambiguous life *at the end of* history. These symbols are an extension of the quest for unambiguous life, but they take up the dimension of history.

Tillich restates the three processes of life: self-integration, self-creativity, and self-transcendence. These processes all drive toward fulfillment in unambiguous life. History in these processes points to the harmony of power and justice, the creation of new being, and the universal fulfillment of potential being. History actualizes some of these potentialities through its quests, and these result in the ambiguities of history. In other words, there is an innate striving for the fulfillment of history that impacts history. The striving for an ideal society, for new being, for the realization of potentials—all this leads to concrete ambiguities such as empire-building, revolutions, and the demonic. These are false or partial fulfillments of history that nonetheless bear a trace of the striving toward ultimate fulfillment. They are a result of the striving for the Kingdom of God and Eternal Life, and thus point to a question that can only be answered by these symbols.

However, these strivings are not entirely discarded. Instead, they are affirmed as questions that long for a fulfillment that can only arrive by grace. The example of false kingdoms in the form of imperial history is instructive. Empire-building is a striving towards unambiguous history, but while it anticipates that history, it nevertheless fails to transcend its own ambiguity. These attempts are an example of the quest for unambiguous life in and beyond history, which is answered by the Christian message of the Kingdom and Eternal Life. But just as Spiritual Presence does not negate the structure of human spirit, so Tillich accepts the reality that social movements for human freedom, justice, and love are not negated completely even if the Kingdom transcends them. The relationship is dialectical.

The Kingdom of God bears both an "inner-historical and a transhistorical side" (ST3, 357). The former is "manifest" through the symbol of Spiritual Presence, while the latter is "identical" with Eternal Life. Thus, the symbol is, for Tillich, "a most important and most difficult symbol of Christian thought…" (ST3, 357). Tillich then describes four characteristics of the Kingdom of God symbol: the political, social, personal, and universal. These reflect the conviction that the symbol is "immanent and transcendent at the same time" (ST3, 359). It is an error to emphasize either dimension without the other.

The Kingdom of God symbolizes the power of salvation and healing, which "breaks into history, works through history, but is not created by history" (ST3, 363). The central manifestation of the Kingdom is Jesus the Christ, who manifests the New Being. By "center," Tillich means that this moment, the appearance of Christ, is the center of history insofar as "everything before and after is both preparation and reception" (ST3, 364).

How does the Kingdom of God relate to the church? Tillich writes instructively, "[W]e can say that church history is at no point identical with the Kingdom of God and at no point without manifestations of the Kingdom of God" (ST3, 378). Likewise, just as the Kingdom of God cannot be identified with the church, so it cannot be identified with any political institution or movement. At the same time, many movements contain trace hints of the Kingdom in anticipation of its fulfillment. But any attempt to absolutize a movement, ideology, or political reality leads to the demonic, that is, a false ultimate. "Demonic consequences result from absolutizing the fragmentary fulfilment of the aim of history within history" (ST3, 390).

Tillich holds together both the inner and transhistorical characteristics in order to avoid this demonization. There are fragmentary victories within history, signs of the Kingdom, but these are not absolute fulfillments. There is then a tension that allows space for experimentation and mistakes in manifesting the Kingdom within history, while also safeguarding against any efforts to absolutize any concrete manifestation. There can be no political, social, personal, or universal manifestation that is either identified with *or* completely removed from the Kingdom of God. There is only the quest for unambiguous life that is symbolized by the Kingdom of God in its inner-historical and transhistorical dimensions.

Eternal Life

The Kingdom of God within history points toward its fulfillment at the end of history, and Tillich uses the symbol of "Eternal Life" to talk about this end. "The end of history in the sense of the inner aim or the *telos* of history is 'eternal life'" (ST3, 394). Just as Tillich stressed how Spiritual Presence is not the negation of human spirit, so he emphasizes that the end of history is not the negation of history but "the elevation of the temporal into eternity" (ST3, 396). This point gives "eternal life" its relevance for the present moment: "[W]e stand *now* in face of the eternal, but we do so looking ahead toward the end of history and the end of all which is temporal in the eternal" (ST3, 396). The relation of history to Eternal Life is one of elevation, not negation. Tillich writes about the Kingdom of God symbol:

> Its basic assertion is that the ever present end of history elevates the positive content of history into eternity at the same time that it excludes the negative from participation in it. Therefore nothing which has been created in history is lost, but it is liberated from the negative with which it is entangled within existence.[11]

Eternal Life is then the liberation of history from its ambiguities; it is the fulfillment of the potentialities of being. This connects history to eternity more directly than most concepts of an abstract "afterlife." Eternal Life is not *another* life but *this life* elevated beyond its ambiguities. Tillich explains, "What happens in time and space, in the smallest particle of matter as well as in the greatest personality, is significant for the eternal life. And since eternal life is participation in the divine life, every finite happening is significant for God" (ST3, 398). The ultimate judgment is then the destruction of the negatives of history, a burning fire the purifies and elevates history to its fulfillment in unambiguous life—"nothing that has being can be ultimately annihilated" (ST3, 399). Julian of Norwich famously writes in a similar frame of mind, "Sin was unavoidable. But all shall be well, and all shall be well, and absolutely everything shall be well."[12]

We should take careful note of the fact that Eternal Life, for Tillich, is not a "a future state of things." Instead, "It is always present, not only in man (who is aware of it), but also in everything that has being within the whole of being" (ST3, 400). Eternal Life is not an "afterlife," but the

---

11. Paul Tillich, ST3, 397.
12. Julian of Norwich, *All Shall Be Well* trans. Ellyn Sanna (Vestal, New York: 2018), 124-5. Vision thirteenth, chapter twenty-seven.

fulfillment and healing of this life. God triumphs over the ambiguities of life.

We have already discussed the personal dimension of Eternal Life in chapter three as it relates to the doctrine of Christ and New Being. The two symbols considered here—the Kingdom of God and Eternal Life—point to the fulfillment of ambiguous life and history. These reflect both a fulfillment to come and a reality that is present here and now.

Tillich's eschatology pushes the notion of salvation as healing to its completion with the concept of unambiguous life. The world in all its beauty is affirmed, while its evils are overcome. Life finally triumphs over death, love over injustice, and being over nonbeing. This hope leads to a radical affirmation of life here and now. We do not expect *another life* but the elevation of this life. And that makes this life eternally relevant.

Tillich's concept of universal "essentialization," which we discussed in chapter three, unites salvation with healing as a return to our essential nature beyond the ambiguities of life. It is a vision of salvation that is far more participatory, humanizing, and life-affirming than the traditional notions of the afterlife as life in an ethereal place called "heaven." While Tillich does affirm the continuation of self-consciousness, his vision of Eternal Life is far more holistic and embracing than escapist visions. Human life and history in all its complexity are lifted up, healed, and included into the divine life and love of God.

It is noteworthy that Tillich's focus is on what we are saved *for* (i.e, unambiguous life), instead of fixating on what we are saved *from* (i.e., hell). The gospel we preach today often implies that God saves us from the threat of what God will do to us if we do not accept salvation. In Tillich's vision, however, the last judgment is an act of *healing,* not an arbitrary punishment to satisfy God's bloodlust. Just as a surgeon must cut out cancer cells from the body, so judgment involves the removal of the negatives in life for the purpose of elevating life and history into the divine presence. On the last day, history and life are *affirmed,* not rejected, by God's healing judgment; and therefore, all things will participate in the divine life so that God will be "all in all" (1 Cor. 15:28).

Sermon: Nothing Real is Lost or Forgotten

In a fascinating sermon on "forgetting and being forgotten," based on Philippians 3:13, Tillich examines positive and negative types of forgetting. There is the liberating type of forgetting that frees us from the burden of the past and its guilt. In this sense, it can be a gift. It can be liberating to forget not only because it gives permission to move on, but because it also means freedom from the painful effects of the past upon the present. This kind of forgetting is traditionally known as "repentance." It involves turning away from the pain of past guilt and moving toward a new life.

Repentance is sometimes marred with connotations of shame and despair, but Tillich recaptures its positive meaning and explains how it is more properly understood as "liberating forgetfulness."[1] He writes how "originally it meant a 'turning around,' leaving behind the wrong way and turning toward the right."[2] That does not mean we simply repress the past and move on, of course. Rather, we have to acknowledge our guilt, yet, *in spite of* it, we accept the liberating message of acceptance by grace. Repentance, then, is the positive type of forgetting, a liberating forgetfulness that helps us accept our participation in New Being in Christ.

---

1. Paul Tillich, *The Eternal Now* (New York: Charles Scribner's Sons, 1963), 31.
2. Ibid.

However, there is also a negative side to forgetfulness. This aspect is connected to the anxiety of death, which is the fear of being forgotten and lost to time. We are prone to repress the fear of death, but it is always with us as finite creatures. And a central element in the anxiety we feel is the fear of being lost and forgotten. Within a generation or two, most of us will be entirely forgotten. And that terrifies us. For Tillich, it is not our fear of the act of dying itself that causes anxiety; "No, in the depth of the anxiety of having to die is the anxiety of being eternally forgotten."[3] It is Tillich's conviction that the Christian message answers this anxiety with the message of Eternal Life.

Tillich concludes his sermon by proclaiming the comforting word that nothing will be lost or forgotten:

> Nothing truly real is forgotten eternally, because everything real comes from eternity and goes to eternity.... Nothing real is absolutely lost and forgotten. We are together with everything real in the divine life. Only the unreal, in us and around us, is pushed into the past forever. This is what 'last judgment' means—to separate in us, as in everything, what has true and final being from what is merely transitory and empty of true being. We are never forgotten, but much in us that we liked and for which we longed may be forgotten forever. Such judgment goes on in every moment of our lives, but the process is hidden in time and manifest only in eternity. Therefore, let us push into the past and forget what should be forgotten forever, and let us go forward to that which expresses our true being and cannot be lost in eternity.[4]

Tillich makes the distinction between real and unreal being, and argues that real being has its foundation in the "ground of being," that is, God, and therefore, there is eternal remembrance in the divine life. The last judgment entails liberation from the unreal being, from our estranged and alienated existence. Eternal Life is unambiguous life in the New Being, life that participates in the divine life. Because our true being is

---

3. Ibid., 33.
4. Ibid., 35.

Sermon: Nothing Real is Lost or Forgotten

rooted in God, we are eternally known by God and participate in the power and ground of Being itself.

This sermon directly correlates the anxious question about being forgotten eternally in death with the Christian answer of Eternal Life in the God who triumphs over nonbeing. It is a hope that produces a more deeply existential affirmation of life, as opposed to a cheap escapist hope for heaven. It is a comforting message, but does not try to say too much. Tillich never engaged in idle speculation about an "afterlife." Instead, he responded to the anxiety of finitude with the Christian message of life in the divine life.

This sermon also highlights Tillich's eschatology of universal essentialization, where New Being recaptures our essential being while our existential estrangement is overcome. The negatives of life and history are removed while the positives are elevated to eternal blessedness. Tillich is intentionally vague with his language. He captures a core hope in the Christian doctrine of resurrection, but he avoids the problems that often come with an escapist eschatology that downplays the events of history by retaining the "in spite of" character of grace. The two kinds of forgetting he explores in this sermon explain this tension well; we will forget that which hinders our essential being, but we will not forget that which is true to our essential being as it is found in the eternal life of God. Nothing *real* will be lost or forgotten.

Sidebar: The Trinity

Tillich, like Schleiermacher, considers the trinitarian symbols toward the end of his system, not to downplay its significance, but because this placement better reflects an existential understanding of the Christian doctrine of God. In other words, Tillich considers the Trinity only *after* christology and pneumatology (doctrines of Christ and the Spirit) because that is how the symbol developed existentially. This reflects Tillich's conviction that the Christian message answers questions implied in our situation. Therefore, he tries to think about the Trinity not as a speculative doctrine but as a reality that is existentially relevant to us. That arguably makes the Trinity *more* necessary for the Christian message than if it were merely a doctrine we are forced to rehearse because it is orthodox. Instead, it is here treated seriously as a necessary part of the Christian message because it answers the human situation of sin and estrangement. Tillich explains, "Like every theological symbol, the trinitarian symbolism must be understood as an answer to the questions implied in man's predicament" (ST3, 285). In contrast, Tillich thinks Karl Barth's placement of the Trinity at the beginning of his *Church Dogmatics* was a "mistake" because it risks suggesting that the "doctrine falls from heaven" instead of being existentially relevant to the human situation (ST3, 285).

So what, then, is Tillich's concept of the Trinity? For Tillich, the Trinity is *dialectical,* which means the symbols "reflect the dialectics of life, namely the movement of separation and reunion" (ST3, 284). When the Trinity was reduced to the nonsensical assertion that three is one and one is three, it lost its existential power. Instead of this "trick" of "numerical identity," Tillich argues that the doctrine describes "a real process" (ST3, 284-5). The process of separation and reunion that describes all life is then applied to the Divine life "in symbolic terms," and that is the origin of the doctrine of the Trinity (ST3, 285).

The existential questions that are answered by the trinitarian symbol are summarized by the three parts of Tillich's *Systematic Theology*. He writes:

> Man's predicament, out of which the existential questions arise, must be characterized by three concepts: finitude with respect to man's esential [sic] being as creature, estrangement with respect to man's existential being in time and space, ambiguity with respect to man's participation in life universal. The questions arising out of man's finitude are answered by the doctrine of God and the symbols used in it [ST1]. The questions arising out of man's estrangement are answered by the doctrine of the Christ and the symbols applied to it [ST2]. The questions arising out of the ambiguities of life are answered by the doctrine of the Spirit and its symbols [ST3]. Each of these answers expresses that which is a matter of ultimate concern in symbols derived from particular revelatory experiences. Their truth lies in their power to express the ultimacy of the ultimate in all directions. The history of the trinitarian doctrine is a continuous fight against formulations which endanger this power.[1]

This provides us with a helpful blueprint of Tillich's system, but it also demonstrates the profound trinitarian structure of his theology. Without naming the Trinity directly, Tillich has been guiding us to this point with each preceding volume. It is also important to notice that Tillich does not claim that the Trinity *derives* from the existential question. Rather, it is from "particular revelatory experiences." The doctrine is a matter of revelation, not a projection from the human question up into God. There is a

---

1. Paul Tillich, ST3, 285-6.

Sidebar: The Trinity

real sense in which God is triune, but what Tillich is trying to show is how this correlates with our existential situation under the categories of being, existence, and life.

The Trinity originally expressed "the self-manifestation of God to man, opening up the depth of the divine abyss and giving answers to the question of the meaning of existence" (ST3, 291). However, the doctrine later became "an impenetrable mystery, put on the altar, to be adored" (ST3, 291). It was then treated like a riddle or an irrational paradox, which lost its existential power to speak directly to our situation. The average Christian in the pew on Sunday only thinks about the Trinity as an abstract doctrine they subscribe to, instead of thinking about it as a reality that is relevant to their lives.

Thus, Tillich, like Schleiermacher before him, argues that the doctrine of the Trinity is in dire need of reconsideration. As it stands, the danger of losing its existential power is due to how this dogma has been treated as a riddle to be solved. The number "three" is not "decisive in trinitarian thinking," but rather, what is central to affirm "the unity in a manifoldness of divine self-manifestations" (ST3, 293). The language we employ around the Trinity often falls back into superstitious and irrational thought, as if the dogma were merely a mystery.

In this regard, Tillich is remarkably sensitive to some of the concerns later raised by feminist theologians regarding the masculine naming of God. In place of the traditional doctrine of the Trinity, Tillich suggests a few lines of development, which directly respond to the difficulties of gendering God. In terms of God the Father, Tillich suggests an emphasis on God as the "ground of being," which "points to the mother-quality of giving birth, carrying, and embracing, and, at the same time, of calling back, resisting independence of the created, and swallowing it" (ST3, 293-4). In terms of the Logos manifested in Christ, Tillich suggests the symbol of self-sacrifice of "finite particularity which transcends the alternative male-female" (ST3, 294). The symbol of self-sacrifice "breaks the contrast of the sexes" (ST3, 294). Finally, in terms of the Holy Spirit, Tillich suggests the "ecstatic character of the Spiritual Presence which transcends the alternative of male and female symbolism in the experience of the Spirit" (ST3, 294). Thus, Tillich offers an alternative to a patriarchal model of God, while also offering a few constructive lines for thinking about the Trinity today.

Ultimately, Tillich hopes to retain the existential relevance of the trinitarian symbols without forcing the acceptance of the Trinity as an irrational or paradoxical mystery. Tillich's goal is to maintain the existential power of the doctrine while revising its more problematic points. Ultimately, he argues that the doctrine must remain open:

> The doctrine of the Trinity is not closed. It can be neither discarded nor accepted in its traditional form. It must be kept open in order to fulfil its original functions—to express in embracing symbols the self-manifestation of the Divine Life to man.[2]

Tillich's entire theological system is an attempt to develop the Trinity along these lines: forgoing the traditional form while retaining its original function (and power). Ultimately, whatever we might make of Tillich's approach, it is worth acknowledging that his goal of making the Trinity existentially relevant, to move it away from needless superstition and irrational speculation, is a worthy challenge for future trinitarian theologies. Since Tillich's challenge, many have already conducted this work in innovative and interesting ways, leading to a renaissance in Trinitarian thinking.[3] In this way, Tillich's insight has proven to be prophetic.

Furthermore, the familiar pattern, which we have often noted, of union-estrangement-reunion is once again central to Tillich's thought. This point connects the Trinity with divine love in a profound way. God is triune because God is the love that reunites what has been estranged. The unity of being is rooted in God as the ground and power of being—the first person of the Trinity. The New Being overcomes the estrangement of being manifest in Jesus as the Christ, the second person of the Trinity. And the reunion of the estranged is the fulfillment of unambiguous life through the symbol of Spiritual Presence, the third person of the Trinity. Tillich's system is thus a profound exploration of the belief that God is love and God is triune.

---

2. Paul Tillich, ST3, 294.
3. For example, Jürgen Moltmann's social trinitarianism, Leonardo Boff's liberative concept of the Trinity as a social program, Elizabeth Johnson's feminist theology, and Sallie McFague's ecological model. These theologians—among others—have developed the Trinity in a way that recovers its existential relevance to the human situation.

5. The Method of Correlation

Summary: Paul Tillich's method of correlation reflects the *incarnational structure, christological center,* and *soteriological telos* of his theology. This method is a theological statement about the incarnate Word that has reached us in our situation. It is incarnational in structure by uniting, without confusion, the Christian message and the existential questions of the situation. It is christologically centered because the norm of this theology is Jesus the Christ, who reunites the estranged. And it bears a soteriological *telos* (goal/end) in its basic claim that the New Being manifested in Jesus the Christ brings healing to our situation both now and in the eschaton. Tillich's method is not *speculative,* then, but profoundly incarnational, christological, and soteriological.

In Tillich's own words:

> The Gospel is by its very definition transcendent, from beyond the world. But at the same time it is a message *to* me; I must receive it; it must concern me in my very existence and in my world. I must understand it,

my existence must be transformed by it. Therefore it is immanent, it belongs to my world.[1]

You could talk about God without talking of man only if God were an object beside others, but that is exactly what all prophetic religion denies. You cannot talk about him except in the situation of correlation with him.[2]

[T]here is no contrast between Socrates and Paul.[3]

Secondary Quotes:

As you believe him, so you have him.[4]

— Martin Luther

For Tillich, to do theology is to be situated: the truth of theology is based in a particular time.[5]

— Oswald Bayer

Tillich was a dialectical thinker who interpreted the gospel in light of the modern situation and the modern situation in light of the gospel. He called this the "method of correlation."[6]

— Carl E. Braaten

---

1. Paul Tillich, *The Ground of Being*, ed. Robert M. Price (Mindvendor, 2015), 78.
2. Ibid., 218.
3. Paul Tillich, ST1, 96.
4. Martin Luther, quoted in Tillich ST1, 61n.
5. Oswald Bayer, "Tillich as Systematic Theologian" in *The Cambridge Companion to Paul Tillich*, ed. Russel Re Manning (Cambridge: Cambridge University Press, 2009), 18.
6. Carl E. Braaten, "Paul Tillich's Message for Our Time," in *Anglican Theological Review* 72-1 (1990), 17.

The Method of Correlation

Introduction

Tillich's method of correlation is crucial for understanding his theology as a whole. So why consider it only now? I wanted to build up to an understanding of the method of correlation rather than begin with it because Tillich claims there is an essential unity between method and content. He explains, "Method and system determine each other" (ST1, 60), and "Methodological awareness always follows the application of a method; it never precedes it" (ST1, 34). I interpret these remarks to mean that the method of correlation is best understood *after* considering the content of the system. Even though Tillich considers his method first in the introduction—necessarily—a clear understanding of the method is not found in its abstract description but in its concrete use.

Accordingly, each chapter has been leading up to this point, where we can arrive at a full appreciation of the method of correlation. Here, I will articulate directly what this method entails. My reading is unique, but it is designed to fulfill the heuristic goal of helping new readers understand Tillich's thought. This reading provides a framework for thinking about Tillich, one that has helped me come to terms with his work, and hopefully the same will be said for my readers. But this is merely an entry point for thinking about correlation, not a restrictive box.

In brief, I interpret the method of correlation according to its *incarnational structure, christological center,* and *soteriological telos*. I've alluded to each of these claims in previous chapters, but here I will explain the correlation method more directly in terms of these characteristics.

Content and Method

This reading interprets Tillich's method as entirely theological, that is, as a method developed in close relationship with his theological commitments. This approach is in contrast with some readings of the method that interpret it as philosophical or speculative. There is, of course, no contradiction between philosophy and theology, but that unity is a *theological* commitment—one that could only be arrived at through theonomous thinking.

The correlation method relies on an essential unity between philosophy and theology. This unity, like that of religion and culture in theonomy, is *eschatological*. Theonomy anticipates the Kingdom of God, while correlation anticipates an eschatological unity of philosophy and theology, of being and meaning. The now and not yet quality of Tillich's thought that we noted in the previous chapter is relevant here. The method of correlation is based on an eschatological concern that nonetheless influences the present situation—it is *now* and *not yet*. Tillich writes, "I could say that in a perfect theonomy the philosophical analysis of the structure of being-itself would be united with a theological expression of the meaning of being for us. The idea of theonomy requires such an eschatological vision."[7]

Therefore, this eschatological unity is *partially* fulfilled through a correlation method that unites philosophy and theology in the present. Tillich writes, "The mutual immanence of theology and philosophy, though never perfect, is a partially fulfilled eschatology."[8] This correlation is imperfect here and now, but in anticipation of its fulfillment in unambiguous life, there is a partial fulfillment of this unity; "the eschatological unity of theology and philosophy must also have a present actuality, however fragmentarily."[9] This partial actuality is expressed by every theological effort to speak the Christian message according to the philosophical structures of being (which is unavoidable in order for any theology to be intelligible). The unity of *being* (philosophically analyzed) and *meaning* (theologically analyzed) is central to this approach. Thus, the possibility of a correlation method is founded upon this eschatological unity, but that unity is a theological claim. Thus, the method is not a result of philosophical speculation but is closely related to Tillich's theological commitments.

This unity is also why, historically speaking, there has always been a close relationship between theology and philosophy. Theologians must make use of the philosophical concepts available to them from their situation, whether they acknowledge this indebtedness or not. Each theologian then "correlates" theological content, derived from the norms of faith, to speak in a way that is intelligible to their situation. In essence, that is also Tillich's aim with the method of correlation, but he develops it more explicitly than theologians did previously. But it is noteworthy that Tillich

---

7. Paul Tillich, "Reply to Interpretation and Criticism," *The Theology of Paul Tillich*, ed. Charles W. Kegley and Robert W. Bretall (New York: The Macmillan Company, 1952), 336.
8. Ibid.
9. Ibid.

The Method of Correlation

thinks this method is not original to his work but a procedure he shares with many theologians throughout church history.

I think this point is worth taking seriously. In the introduction to ST, Tillich suggests that the first sections of John Calvin's *Institutes of the Christian Religion* express "the essence of the method of correlation" (ST1, 63). For Calvin, there can be no knowledge of God without knowledge of the self, and no knowledge of the self without knowledge of God. The first sentence of the *Institutes* reflects this: "Nearly all the wisdom we possess, that is to say, true and sound wisdom, consists of two parts: the knowledge of God and of ourselves."[10] Tillich's correlation method, which has been frequently criticized, is, in fact, a method he thought could be reasonably traced back throughout the history of Christian theology, particularly in Calvin.

The eschatological unity of philosophy and theology means that theology and philosophy must exist in a relationship of "mutual immanence." So, we might also point to how the early church borrowed concepts from Platonic and Neo-Platonic philosophy to speak of the Logos manifested in Jesus, who is the Christ, in a way that was relevant to their time. Or how medieval theologians, especially Thomas Aquinas, synthesized Aristotelian philosophy with Christian theology. Or again, how Schleiermacher, in the nineteenth century, presented the Christian faith in terms relevant to the situation of enlightenment reason and German romanticism by meeting the epistemological challenge set forth by Immanuel Kant. In each period of church history, theologians employed the conceptual tools at their disposal to proclaim the Christian message anew to their situation.

However, it is crucial to clarify that theology's use of these philosophical tools does not imply *subjugating* the Christian faith to philosophy. The relationship is one of unity, not dominance. Neither Platonism nor Aristotelianism nor the Enlightenment can determine the content of Christian faith, even if these philosophies remain indispensable for explaining that message. This conviction is central to the correlation method and Tillich's use of existential philosophy and ontology for his analysis of the situation.

---

10. John Calvin, *Institutes of the Christian Religion,* ed. John T. McNeill trans. Ford Lewis Battles (Philadelphia: The Westminster Press, 1960), 35.

My point is this: Tillich's approach is far more orthodox than often thought. There is historical precedent for his correlation method, and Tillich consciously follows the tradition while developing it in his own way. Tillich's strength lies in how consistently he reflects on and implements his method, but as a method, it is one he finds consistent with traditional approaches of systematic theology historically.

The goal in this section has been to take Tillich seriously when he directly says that the method of correlation is a "theological assertion" (ST1, 8). The method is descriptive, then, of a theology that presupposed that the Word of God speaks to us still today as the Spirit opens our ears to receive the message of New Being. In other words, the core conviction of this method is that God's Word has become flesh and dwelt among us. The eschatological unity of philosophy (questions of being) and theology (answers of revelation) is a core element in Tillich's incarnational, christological, and soteriological method of correlation. We will now turn to more specific descriptions of the method to understand it as charitably as possible.

Incarnational Structure

Tillich's system is structurally incarnational. What I mean is that, at its core, his method relies on an original union between the divine and human. The very structure of the system reveals this fact by correlating the human situation with the Christian message in a way that brings together the questions of being with the answer of the Christian message in the categories of reason/revelation, being/God, existence/Christ, life/Spiritual Presence, and history/Kingdom of God. This structure traces the reality of a God who is present in the human situation and builds upon that foundational claim.

A consistent motif that runs throughout Tillich's theology illustrates this well: the pattern of union-estrangement-reunion. At its core, Tillich's theology is about the essential *union* of God and humanity, the existential *estrangement* of humanity from God, and the now-and-not-yet *reunion* of God and humanity in the New Being revealed in Jesus the Christ. The system, then, reflects this movement structurally through the method of correlation.

The traditional approach to the unity of God and humanity in Christ

The Method of Correlation

was articulated by the Chalcedonian Formula in the fifth century, which is still considered a foundational orthodox christological statement. The Definition established a hypostatic union of God and humanity in Jesus, confessing that there is one Son, the self-same perfect God, and the self-same perfect human, truly God and man, co-essential with the Father and humanity. Jesus Christ was a human being exactly like us in all things except for sin; two unconfused natures in the one person. Those are the basic claims of the Chalcedonian Definition.

A similar logic is at work with Tillich's method of correlation; he aims to bring together, without confusion, the Christian message and the human situation. The message is divinely originated and knowable through revelation (though it is *received* humanly), while the human situation is known through a philosophical analysis of being. There is a dialectical back-and-forth that then takes place between philosophical analysis and theology. The basic claim of Tillich's system, then, is that the Word has truly become flesh, that the message speaks directly in and through the conceptual tools of the human situation, which leads him to develop a twofold analysis of situation and message.

Tillich first describes the method by stating that every theology must satisfy two requirements, "the statement of the truth of the Christian message and the interpretation of this truth for every new generation" (ST 1, 3). That necessitates moving "back and forth" between the foundational truth of the Christian message and the temporal situation in which it is received. Tillich then describes how the method of correlation functions: "It makes an analysis of the human situation out of which the existential questions arise, and it demonstrates that the symbols used in the Christian message are the answers to these questions" (ST 1, 62). Or in other words, "The Christian message provides the answers to the questions implied in human existence" (ST 1, 64). Tillich's theology proclaims that the Christian message has become flesh and meets us in our situation. The analysis of being is based on the conviction that God speaks the word of grace and New Being *to us* in our time and space, and in terms we can understand within our present situation.

There is a dialectical character to this method. Tillich correlates the message and the situation, but he is quick to remind us that the message is received through imperfect mediums. God reveals Godself to us, but our reception of the message of New Being is never in a vacuum but is always received in our limited situation as finite beings. Thus, it is not necessarily a "divine" message that is correlated with the human situation. The message originates from the ultimate, but it is received humanly, and thus, there can be no illusions about the message of Christian faith becoming a kind of divine oracle free from the unavoidable reception of that message through culture, language, and philosophy. In this sense, Tillich is deeply committed to divine revelation, but he is clear that revelation is not "thrown like a stone" from heaven, but truly reaches us, which means it is expressed through imperfect, human mediums. If that were not the case, then we would not know revelation. That is why, in part one of the system, Tillich correlates reason and revelation, which we will consider below.

Answering Theology

In this light, Tillich's concept of an "answering" theology becomes clear. Apologetic theology is a dangerous term that implies a fraught history of fundamentalist attacks on modernity—against science, philosophy, psychology, etc.—and a general posture of arrogance in the Christian witness. Still, it is a risk Tillich is willing to take because of his conviction that theology must state the message and interpret it for each new situation. The plethora of misreadings surrounding Tillich's theology as an anthropological projection or a speculative philosophy is perhaps due to this risk. But why, then, does Tillich think it is necessary to use this term?

Tillich outlines two errors, again in an incarnational fashion. First, the error of a purely kerygmatic theology is to deny any common ground outside of the theological circle. This implies that the divine Word has no commonality with the human situation. Thus, kerygmatic theology often critiques apologetic theologians as surrendering the kerygma (message) to the human situation. That means the situation cannot be taken seriously, and the task of theology is simply resigned to throwing the divine message like a stone from heaven at the human situation (ST1, 7). But Tillich insists that this is a naive approach. Even kerygmatic theologians must use the conceptual tools at their disposal, or else they would be unintelligible. They cannot escape being humans bound by the limitations of history, culture, and finitude. Thus, "theology cannot escape the problem of the situation" (ST1, 7). Tillich's recommendation to kerygmatic theology is to abandon its exclusive transcendence and take seriously the "attempt of apologetic theology to answer the questions put before it by the contemporary situation" (ST1, 7). The underlying claim is that theology cannot be solely "divine" but must also be human. That is a theological claim, at its core.

This critique was directed toward Karl Barth and so-called neo-orthodoxy. And while this critique has been challenged by Barth scholars (and I would echo that challenge),[11] the overall argument about kerygmatic theology is still relevant today against versions of fundamentalism that refuse to consider the limitations of those who received the message, even in the biblical texts. Instead, the Bible is perceived as a purely divine message without any corresponding human response. But this turns the Bible, in Tillich's terminology, into a demonic force. The claim of Wayne Grudem and other American evangelicals to engage in an undiluted "biblical theology," which ignores any human situation and merely repeats supposed eternal truths fossilized in Scripture, is an example of this danger. This approach to theology can and often is used as an oppressive force against liberation and healing, effectively flipping the Christian message on its head. That is the danger of a purely kerygmatic theology.

But apologetic theology also has its risks. Tillich admits there is some truth in the warning about apologetics losing "itself if it is not based on the kerygma as the substance and criterion of each of its statements" (ST1, 7). In other words, a purely human theology (situational) risks losing the Christian message. That once again reflects an incarnational structure to Tillich's approach. He aims to unite the kerygmatic with the apologetic while emphasizing the necessity of the "answering" function of theology.

Tillich's emphasis on an answering theology was thus a pragmatic decision based on what he recognized as the urgent task of theology for his time. He suggests, revealingly, that perhaps in other times another approach would be necessary. Interestingly, Tillich thought that Barth's theology was "more appropriate" for the Second World War and the timely task of fighting against tyrants. In the long run, however, Tillich

---

11. See, for example, Bruce McCormack's explanation of why the term "neo-orthodoxy" is faulty: *Karl Barth's Critically Realistic Dialectical Theology* (Oxford: Clarendon Press, 1995), 1-28. The term is based more on the American reception of Barth than Barth himself.

believed he was right about theology and culture and the need for an answering theology after the war.[12] But this comment is instructive. Tillich did not seem to think that his approach was *the* universal way to do theology, but the necessary one for his time and situation. That shows how seriously Tillich understood theology's role as a timely discipline.

A primary reason for his decision has to do with the irrelevance of Christian symbols for the modern individual. For example, Tillich reflects on the fact that both the symbols "God" and "sin" have become almost meaningless for his time. That is confirmed whenever someone asks, "Does God exist?" Tillich explains, "Now the very asking of the question signifies that the symbols of God have become meaningless. For God, in the question, has become one of innumerable objects in time and space which may or may not exist. And this is not the meaning of God at all."[13] Furthermore, sin has become a symbol for "a particular act which contradicts conventional moralities, especially when it refers to sex."[14] Tillich prefers "estrangement" to sin for this reason. Thus, Tillich's theology strives to interpret "religious symbols in such a way that the secular [person]... can understand and be moved by them."[15] That is the motivation behind Tillich's decision to engage in an answering theology despite the acknowledged risks.

But ultimately, Tillich writes that "kerygmatic theology needs apologetic theology for its completion" (ST 1, 6). This move toward a dialectical relationship is central—which Tillich consciously attempts in lineage with Schleiermacher's great system.[16] With the method of correlation,

---

12. He confessed to Langdon Gilkey, "[When] you're fighting against a tyrant, [then] Barth is [the] best man to have on your side.... Barth's message was appropriate for [that] *kairos*—more appropriate [than] mine. I respect and have always respected Barth, not only for the originality and power of his theology but also for the clarify of his insight into the idolatry of Hitler and his courage for declaring it. But, I was *right* about the relation of culture to theology, even a theology of resistance against culture, and Barth was wrong, even about his own 'revelation theology' which is *full* of culture." Langdon Gilkey, *Gilkey on Tillich* (New York: The Crossroad Publishing Company, 1990), 204.
13. Paul Tillich, *Ultimate Concern: Tillich in Dialogue,* ed. D. Mackenzie Brown, (New York: Harper & Row, Publishers, 1965), 88.
14. Ibid.
15. Ibid., 88-9.
16. Paul Tillich, *A History of Christian Thought,* ed. Carl E. Braaten (New York: Touchstone Books, 1968), 387.

then, Tillich tries to avoid the dangers of both kerygmatic and apologetic theologies.

It is vital, however, to recognize the orthodoxy in Tillich's approach, contrary to his critics. The difficulty of understanding Tillich today is getting past the plethora of misreadings that make him into a purely speculative, philosophical (or existential) theologian akin to Feuerbach, or as someone who bases the kerygma on projections taken from the human situation and who has, accordingly, lost the Christian message. But this reading fails to recognize the mediating quality of Tillich's approach, which is structurally rooted in a incarnational logic that unites, without confusion, the divine message with the human situation.

In other words, Tillich does not "speak of God by speaking of man in a loud voice," which was Barth's critique of Schleiermacher and liberal theology. Instead, he speaks of the incarnate God who has revealed Godself in and through the medium of human conceptual tools. Thus, to speak of God *without* the human situation is to speak of a God who has not *reached us* in our situation. Instead, it is to speak of a distant God, merely an object somewhere else apart from us. Tillich is emphatic that theology must speak of the God who has become incarnate, who is present and active in the existential questions of the situation.

Mystical *a Priori*

There is another conviction in Tillich's theology that might help further illuminate his method. For Tillich, there exists a "mystical a priori"—an awareness of something that transcends both subject and object—which grounds both the idealist and naturalist theological concepts (ST1, 9). The mystical a priori is Tillich's basis for religious consciousness. It refers to the phenomenon of the holy. But theologically, it reflects the original unity between God and creation. The human situation, as we will see below, can ask the question of existence because of the presence of the answer. But methodologically, this a priori presupposes a point of contact between God and humanity, and it manifests in Tillich's method of correlation by stressing the contextual dimension of theological work. Thus, following Luther—"As you believe him so you have him"—Tillich writes, "God in his self-manifestation to man is dependent on the way man receives his manifestation" (ST 1, 61). There is no pure message without the human reception of it. That is not a flaw in theology but reflects the mystical a priori of the divine and human unity. This unity is not only eschatological but a priori, which reflects Tillich's familiar pattern: union-estrangement-reunion.

Tillich describes how this mystical a priori is essentially rooted in Augustine's theology, writing, "God is not an object beside other objects.... Rather, [God] is our own a priori; [God] precedes ourselves in dignity, reality, and logical validity. In [God] the split between the subject and object, and the desire of the subject to know the object, are overcome.... God is given to the subject as nearer to itself than it is to itself."[17] The final sentence is a reference to Augustine's famous saying, "God is nearer to us than our innermost being." It is because God is nearer to the human being than they are to themselves that the divine message and human situation correlate. God as the Ground of Being is the mystical a priori that makes possible and necessary the method of correlation.

Thus, the unity of kerygmatic and apologetic theology is rooted in an original unity of the divine and human. Tillich has this in mind when stressing the need for a method of correlation. The system is possible because this mystical a priori exists, because of the original unity between God and humanity in a state of being beyond subject and object, and in spite of its disruption by human sin. Thus, Tillich rejects the kerygmatic argument that there is no point of contact between the divine and human. As Tillich later articulates, "One belongs essentially to that from which one is estranged" (ST2, 45). Elsewhere, he contrasts the term estrangement with the term *stranger*.[18] A stranger is someone without any connection to the individual, but an *estranged* person implies an essential relationship that has been disrupted. God is not a stranger to humanity; rather, humanity is estranged from the One to whom it belongs essentially. This essential unity is what Tillich has in mind with the mystical a priori.

We might also see this as Tillich's endorsement of the Lutheran claim: *finitum capax infiniti*—the finite is capable of the infinite. This point was a matter of controversy between Lutheran and Reformed theologians, but

---

17. Paul Tillich, *A History of Christian Thought,* ed. Carl E. Braaten (New York: Touchstone Books, 1968), 112.
18. Paul Tillich, *Ultimate Concern: Tillich in Dialogue,* ed. D. Mackenzie Brown, (New York: Harper & Row, Publishers, 1965), 47-8.

The Method of Correlation

Tillich clearly sides with Luther to say that finitude *is* capable of the infinite. The mystical a priori expresses this directly by positing a unity between God and creation that makes possible the finite capacity for the infinite. The ultimate can be received—is *only* received—within the conditions of finitude. That makes the correlation method unavoidable.

Another point to consider in this regard is Tillich's concept of the theological circle. Being inside the circle means the theologian is grasped by faith. Thus, Tillich acknowledges the churchly orientation of theology. But while Tillich is clear that a theologian must be within that circle, he also insists on asking if the Christian message has validity outside it. He emphasizes that this is precisely the task of an answering theology—to establish the validity of the Christian claim to those outside the circle (ST1, 15). That explains his emphasis on the human situation. It is because Tillich is convinced that there is no Godless place where the New Being has not prepared the way for itself, that reason itself contains a logos structure that makes revelation possible, he strives to demonstrate the validity of theology for those outside the circle. While theology lives within the circle, it cannot proceed without constant awareness of those outside the circle who are nonetheless affected by the claims of the Christian message. Theology is a project of those who have faith; in that sense, it is existential. Yet theology is also relevant to those outside of faith; in that sense, it is a science (*Wissenschaft*). Both aspects are brought together in Tillich's approach.

Tillich's basic claim is that the kerygma has truly reached the human situation. That is why, in contrast with purely kerygmatic theology, Tillich upholds a point of contact between the divine and human. This helps explain the great risk Tillich was willing to take with his apologetic approach. Despite the misuse of apologetics, he strived to recapture its original use and apply it today. He is consciously working within the framework of Acts 17, as he explains in a sermon, "The famous scene in which Paul speaks from the central place of Greek wisdom shows us a man who is the prototype of the answering theologian."[19]

According to Tillich, there are three stages to Paul's answering approach. First, "those who ask him the ultimate question are not uncon-

---

19. Paul Tillich, *The Shaking of the Foundations* (New York: Charles Scribner's Sons, 1948), 127.

scious of the answer."[20] This point refers to the mystical a priori that God is closer to the questioner than they are to themselves. Second, Paul's answer reflects the tendency of human beings to pervert God and create idols in an effort to flee from the true God.[21] But there is no reconciliation between idols and God. This echoes Tillich's point about the demonic. Third, and most critically, Paul answers that the Logos has been made manifest in Jesus Christ. It was an answer they could not accept, but it is the vital stage of Paul's response. Yet Tillich does not think the paradox of the Logos manifesting in Jesus should simply be thrown at listeners. At the same time, the paradox cannot be emptied of its power. The message of the New Being is neither collapsed into the situation nor irrelevant to it. The task of a theologian is to interpret the paradox, the message, in a way that is relevant to the situation.

The incarnational structure helps explain the reason why the method of correlation is necessary, but the christological center of Tillich's system demonstrates how this method theologically functions. We will now turn to Tillich's christological center and especially note the soteriological telos of his system to complete this description of the method.

CHRISTOLOGICAL CENTER AND SOTERIOLOGICAL *TELOS*

It is crucial to see how revelation is not just information, for Tillich. So, the question of being is not a question in the ordinary sense of asking for information, but rather, it is a situation seeking to be *healed* by the New Being. It is vital to keep in mind that the "question" for Tillich is the human themselves—it is our life lived under the conditions of finitude, estrangement, and ambiguity. *We* are the question that is answered by the reality of New Being. That is why the method of correlation is christologically centered and soteriologically directed. The method of correlation declares that the divine being has truly overcome human estrangement by positing a New Being from within our situation.

Thus, theological content and soteriological healing go hand in hand with Christ as the center. Tillich's work is a magisterial affirmation of the basic Christian claim that God was in Christ, reconciling the world to

---

20. Ibid.
21. Ibid., 128-9.

The Method of Correlation

Godself; in Christ, there is a new creation (2 Cor. 5:17-19). In that light, it is possible to suggest that Tillich's system is fundamentally soteriological. An answering theology is at once a *healing* theology.

It is also important to see that this is not an *argument* for the New Being. That is something easily missed by Tillich's detailed attention to philosophy and ontology. But it must always be remembered that Tillich rejected the possibility of proving the existence of God. In a sermon, Tillich explains, "No argument of reason can give certainty. The finite cannot argue for the infinite; it cannot reach God and it can never reach its own eternity."[22] We apply the wrong concept of apologetics by reading Tillich as a theologian interested in *proving* the Christian message. His apologetic concern is better explained by the incarnational declaration of the New Being as the healing power to liberate the human situation. That explains the need for an answering theology. It is not information that is central but the proclamation of a reality—a New Being—that truly heals and liberates.

What is the content of the Christian answer? For Tillich, it is the New Being—a reality, not an idea—and it is an answer we could *not* give ourselves. It is a revelation and a gift of grace. Thus, the system is a profoundly evangelical (in the original sense of the word) proclamation that the New Being has truly reached humanity in our situation of blinded reason (pt. 1), finitude under the threat of nonbeing (pt. 2), estrangement from being-itself (pt. 3), life and its ambiguities (pt. 4), and history (pt. 5). The unassumed is the unhealed. That which has been assumed by the New Being is healed: human reason, being, existence, life, and history are met with the God who is for us and with us in Christ. The situation must be correlated with the message because God was in Christ, reconciling the world to Godself. Nothing is excluded from the healing power of the New Being.

These points illustrate the christological center and soteriological *telos* of the method of correlation. The message of Jesus the Christ is central, while the healing power of the New Being is its teleological goal. In this sense, Tillich's system is a remarkable statement about the doctrine of sin and of the Christ who overcomes it. His analysis of the situation is an

---

22. Paul Tillich, *The Shaking of the Foundations* (New York: Charles Scribner's Sons, 1948), 137.

analysis of the "age of anxiety" that is met with the New Being in Christ and the word of grace that we are accepted in spite of being unacceptable. The threats of finitude, estrangement, and ambiguity are met with the message of a God who overcomes, heals, and raises the old into the new.

Correlation Revisited

Therefore, the method of correlation reflects Tillich's broader theological commitments. It is incarnational, christological, and soteriological. In light of this framework, the method of correlation can be fruitfully revisited. Here we will note several important aspects of the method that its critics overlook: First, the question is not the source of the answer. Second, the question is not information but humanity itself. Third, the situation and question can be understood as preserving grace, as creation, which prepares for the answer: grace and the new creation. And that means the question is only possible if the answer is already present with the questioner. This final point is crucial for rightly interpreting correlation.

Tillich clarifies the first and second points in his introduction to ST2. First, he explains that question and answer are independent of each other, which is directed against the misreading that suggests that the answer is derived from the question or vice versa. Instead, the question "is not the source for the revelatory answer formulated by theology. One cannot derive the divine self-manifestation from an analysis of the human predicament. God speaks to the human situation, against it, and for it" (ST2, 13). Even though Tillich thinks it is necessary to begin with the human question, it would be a mistake to think that the question is the basis of the answer or somehow derived from it. He is always careful to stress that the question is limited by the situation of finitude. It faces an uncrossable boundary. The finite question cannot leap into the divine answer. Tillich remains devoted to justification by grace through faith, in that sense, and he plainly states that human beings are unable "to reach God under [their] own power" (ST2, 13). It is also wrong to derive the question from the answer. Thus, he affirms the basic incarnational shape, which takes seriously the fullness of divinity and humanity, the Christian message, and the human situation. Both are taken for what they are and are not flattened into their opposite by the method of correlation.

The Method of Correlation

In connection with this point, Tillich emphasizes that the method of correlation is not what has sometimes been called "natural theology." When natural theology means a natural capability of arriving at the knowledge of God through human means, Tillich rejects it. But Tillich stresses that the traditional meaning of natural theology is "that it gave an analysis of the human situation and the question of God implied in it" (ST2, 14). But it is an "impossible task" to "derive theological affirmation" from the analysis of finitude (ST2, 14). Instead, Tillich affirms that "God is manifest only through God" (ST2, 14). Finally, Tillich explains, "Existential questions and theological answers are independent of each other; this is the first statement implied in the method of correlation" (ST2, 14). Thus, the critique launched against Tillich by Barth and others—that Tillich derives his theology from the human questions—is a misreading of correlation.

Second, Tillich clarifies that the question is not a question among other questions. It is not merely an innocent curiosity raised by impassive observers. It is an *existential* question. He explains, "The question, asked by man, is man himself" (ST2, 13). A person cannot avoid asking the question because the question of existence is synonymous with their very self. This insight is vital for two reasons. First, it further clarifies that the method of correlation is not about deriving theological content from the human question. Second, it reaffirms the soteriological aspect of the system. The correlation is thus between a fallen humanity that cannot escape its situation through its own efforts and the divine answer that is given purely by grace but truly given in and to the human situation.

Third, the method of correlation can be rightly understood only if we see that the question is possible *because* the answer is already present. While Tillich stresses that question and answer are independent of each other, it is nonetheless important to stress that the answer makes the question possible. That does not deny its independence, but rather, indicates a central point often repeated by Tillich, that God is nearer to the subject than the subject is to itself. The question is the human being themselves. Yet to be is to participate in the ground of being through the power of being. Thus, there is no godless questioner to ask the question of being from a distance because there is no being apart from the ground of being.

The answer is grace, a new creation, but this grace does not destroy original creation or nature; it perfects it (Aquinas). Thus, the divine answer may be independent of the question, but the relationship between nature and grace (creation and new creation) is important for understanding the relationship between the question and answer in the method of correlation. This can perhaps be understood in terms of the classic doctrine of a "preceding grace" that prepares and enables a person in their nature to receive salvation. It reflects the original unity of God and humanity despite the estrangement of existence. This concept was first developed by Augustine, who influenced Tillich significantly.

That means the question of being is only possible because of grace, even if it is not enough to arrive at the answer alone. The question of being cannot escape the limitations of finitude. It can never arrive at God's saving and healing knowledge that comes only from the answer. The answer and question remain independent, but they are not incompatible, as if the answer is spoken in a language no one speaks or has the capacity to hear. Yet it must also be grace that we could not give ourselves, a truly divine word.

In this light, Tillich's method takes on even fuller soteriological overtones. His analysis of the existential situation takes seriously the grace present in every human situation. Tillich presupposes that in every situation, God is present as the ground of being and is at work to bring about the New Being to overcome nonbeing. In other words, Tillich astutely observes that there is no questioning apart from the ground of being. Yet prevenient grace is not fully grace, and thus the answer is not derived from the question. A true correlation exists where neither side loses its independence. Yet the possibility of receiving the Christian message is rooted in an analysis of the situation.

All these points have been aimed at revisiting Tillich's method of correlation with an eye toward combating common misunderstandings. Tillich's system is structurally incarnational, christologically centered, and it declares a soteriological telos, namely, that God was in Christ, reconciling the world to Godself.

Test Case: Reason and Revelation

Before concluding, I want to briefly consider the first part of Tillich's system: "reason and revelation." This is Tillich's epistemology, meaning his theory of how we know what we know. So it is highly relevant for under-

The Method of Correlation

standing the method of correlation. It will serve as a sort of "test case" for my interpretation.

For Tillich, the question of reason is an *ontological* question (ST1, 71), not to be mistaken as a quest simply for correct information. Reason reaches its ontological limitation in the quest for the Ultimate. But that limit is not only the inability to provide the right information; it is also the inability to participate in revelation and be liberated by it. Knowledge itself is a form of union: "In every act of knowledge the knower and that which is known are united; the gap between subject and object is overcome" (ST1, 94). Revelation is then a form of salvation, wherein reason participates in its ultimate ground and power. That is why only revelation can answer the quest of reason as it reaches this limit. Therefore, reason needs liberation and healing by the power of revelation, which turns reason into ecstatic reason—i.e., reason that is grasped by revelation.

Revelation does not destroy reason, however. There is no contradiction, just as there was no contradiction between being, existence, history, and life and its fulfillment in God, Christ, the Kingdom, and Eternal Life. Reason is *fulfilled* by revelation. Tillich argues, "Revelation does not destroy reason, but reason raises the question of revelation" (ST1, 81).

Tillich distinguishes between "controlling" and "receiving" knowledge: "[C]ontrolling knowledge is safe but not ultimately significant, while receiving knowledge can be ultimately significant, but it cannot give certainty" (ST1, 105). We discussed in chapter one how faith cannot be equated with certainty. Controlling reason can obtain its object and safely understand it, but receiving knowledge cannot be certain because it is ultimately significant. Revelation (and thus theology) is a form of receiving knowledge; in this regard, it is "a special and extraordinary manifestation which removes the veil from something which is hidden in a special and extraordinary way" (ST1, 108). Or more simply, "Revelation is the manifestation of what concerns us ultimately" (ST1, 110).

Thus, for Tillich, revelation "is invariably revelation for someone in a concrete situation of concern.... There is no revelation 'in general'" (ST1, 111). Revelation is *existential*, in other words. It is not just head-knowledge thrown like a stone from above; it is the fulfillment and liberation of reason. Here, Tillich develops a concept of "ecstatic reason," wherein "the mind is grasped by the mystery, namely, by the ground of being and meaning" (ST1, 112). There is no revelation without ecstasy, which is a state of being outside of one's self, outside of the limits of reason. However, ecstatic reason is still reason. "Ecstasy is not a negation of reason; it is the state of mind in which reason is beyond itself, that is, beyond its subject-object structure" (ST1, 112). Because revelation is the manifestation of an ultimate concern, it is beyond this subject-object structure, even though it is received within the limitations of that structure. Reason is outside of itself because it is grasped by revelation. Tillich writes, "Reason receives revelation in ecstasy and miracles; but reason is not destroyed by revelation, just as revelation is not emptied by reason" (ST1, 118).

How is revelation actually received by reason? For this, Tillich describes "mediums" of revelation, such as Scripture and tradition, but he argues that anything can be a medium. So while Tillich rejects the concept of "natural revelation," he argues that revelation must manifest through natural mediums. Revelation must speak in a language we understand; it becomes incarnate, in other words, in human language and culture. Natural revelation moves in the opposite direction by divinizing the natural. For Tillich, revelation uses human mediums without destroying them, but it remains revelation even in its manifestations. That is why Tillich rejected natural theology and natural revelation. Reason can only ask the questions of being, but the answer is provided by divine revelation, even if it is manifested through natural mediums. Recognizing the movement of this process is essential. Tillich moves from revelation to reason, not the reverse, and he criticizes any movement from reason to revelation. The question of ultimate meaning "is asked by reason, but reason cannot answer it. Revelation can answer it" (ST1, 120).

Tillich further distinguishes between "original" and "dependent" forms of revelation. He uses the example of Jesus: "Jesus is the Christ, both because he could become the Christ and because he was received as the Christ. Without both these sides he would not have been the Christ" (ST1, 126). The church, however, is dependent upon the second form of revelation, on the reception of Jesus as the Christ witnessed to by the first disciples. Therefore, Tillich thinks the church is a place of dependent revelation, not original revelation. That means there is a permanent reference point in Jesus and his reception as the Christ, but no church can claim ownership over original revelation. The church "is the locus of continuous

The Method of Correlation

dependent revelations which are one side of the work of the divine Spirit in the church" (ST1, 127).

The point is to suggest that revelation in the Christian church is always *dependent* revelation. That means revelation is not a *thing* we might possess but a state of reception; it is a state of being grasped by revelation, *not* of grasping it. Tillich writes, "This consideration radically excludes a nonexistential concept of revelation. Propositions about the past revelation give theoretical information; they have no revelatory power.... Revelation, whether it is original or dependent, has revelatory power only for those who participate in it, who enter into the revelatory correlation" (ST1, 127). Revelation is not *information*, but participation in the situation of dependent revelation, wherein reason is grasped by revelation and becomes ecstatic reason. That means revelation is inherently situational because it is the participation in a revelatory power, not the repetition of past manifestations of revelation. Tillich is able to uphold these points without losing either the otherness of revelation and its relatedness to us.

A doctrine that informs Tillich's approach, as we saw in chapter two, is the *analogia entis,* the "analogy of being." This doctrine, for Tillich, "points to the necessity of using material taken from finite reality in order to give content to the cognitive function in revelation" (ST1, 131). Tillich thinks that nothing could be said about God apart from this analogy. In contrast, Barth and other reformed theologians rejected both the *analogia entis* and *finitum capax infiniti* by arguing that finitude is *not* capable of the infinite inherently, but must be *made* capable through grace. For Tillich, in contrast, the basis for our theology is the claim that finitude *is* capable of the infinite. This difference is a central one between these two theologians and their respective traditions (Lutheran and Reformed), but it is important to note in this context. Reason is capable of revelation, for Tillich. That does *not* mean reason can arrive at revelation independently, by its own efforts. Instead, it means that revelation uses our natural reason and does not destroy it, even if it becomes ecstatic reason in the process.

Tillich then considers "actual" revelation, which is Jesus the Christ. He is the final revelation, and no revelation in the church can exist without Christ as its point of reference. The revelation that Jesus is the Christ is the "unsurpassable revelation, that which is the criterion of all others" (ST1, 133). That is the only basis for Christian theology. However, Tillich clarifies, "The unconditional and universal claim of

Christianity is not based on its own superiority over other religions. Christianity, without being final itself, witnesses to the final revelation" (ST1, 134). This point refers back to the difference between original and dependent forms of revelation. The Christian theologian, therefore, exists within a "theological circle" based on the revelation that Jesus is the Christ. Christianity itself is not a final revelation, but it bears witness to a final revelation, namely, Christ. Jesus of Nazareth is the medium for revelation because "he sacrifices himself completely to Jesus as the Christ" (ST1, 136). That logic is essential to Tillich's use of symbols, that a symbol must participate in that which it indicates but also die to itself as a finite symbol.

Revelation, then, is deeply incarnational. It is the state in which reason is grasped by revelation and becomes ecstatic reason. This process is deeply existential. Tillich even suggests that revelation and salvation are two sides of the same coin: "Revelation can be received only in the presence of salvation, and salvation can occur only within a correlation of revelation" (ST1, 144). As a state of being grasped, ecstatic reason is participation in revelation, which is the liberation of reason. Revelation, then, is not attainable by reason working itself up into the ultimate, just as works cannot achieve salvation. Revelation *grasps* reason, not the reverse.

Revelation fulfills reason's ultimate aims. Reason quests for the answers to its ultimate questions, but it cannot answer those questions itself. It can *only* ask the questions of being. Revelation, then, liberates reason from its limitations and transfigures it into ecstatic reason. The logical form of ecstatic reason is *paradox*. Jesus the Christ, who manifests New Being, is a key example. Christ unites "the most concrete of all possible forms of concreteness, a personal life… [and is] the bearer of that which is absolute without condition and restriction" (ST1, 150). Paradox, then, is "the surprising, miraculous, and ecstatic way in which that which is the mystery of being universally is manifest in time, space, and under the conditions of existence, in complete historical concreteness. Final revelation is not logical nonsense; it is a concrete event which on the level of rationality must be expressed in contradictory terms" (ST1, 150-1). This is not, as Tillich notes, the sacrifice of reason. Instead, it is the *fulfillment* of reason. But notably, it is closely related to the paradox of the concrete and absolute. In other words, it is profoundly incarnational,

The Method of Correlation

christological, and soteriological.

The "ground" of revelation is only considered at the end of Tillich's section, but it is vital to the preceding argument. An "apologetic theology" must approach revelation from "below," but after the actuality of revelation is discussed, "the question of the ground of revelation arises" (ST1, 155). Tillich's method forced him to first consider the question of reason before considering the ground of revelation. But, as we have seen, the movement he is describing has its origin in the ground of revelation, which is God. Tillich remains a theologian of grace because reason is liberated by the ground of being, by revelation. The movement he describes is "from above," even if it must be considered "from below."

What is the ground of revelation? It is not its "cause" but the "ground of being" (ST1, 155). Therefore, Tillich comments that such a concept "presupposes the doctrine of Being and God" (ST1, 156). Here, Tillich roots revelation in God as the ground of being that makes possible ecstatic reason. This is possible because God's life is "the dynamic unity of depth and form" (ST1, 156). In other words, the form of reason is not destroyed by revelation because that form is *also* grounded in God's life. That unity is what makes the liberation of finite reason possible to be grasped by revelation.

Tillich's term for the depth of the divine life is the "Abyss," which describes the ineffable character of God. But there is also a structural element to the divine life, which is called "Logos." The unity of both the depth and form is "Spirit." This insight points to a trinitarian structure inherent in revelation. Tillich writes:

> Theologians must use all three terms [Abyss, Logos, Spirit] in order to point to the ground of revelation. It is the abysmal character of the divine life which makes revelation mysterious; it is the logical character of the divine life which makes the revelation of mystery possible; and it is the spiritual character of the divine life which creates the correlation of miracle and ecstasy in which revelation can be received. Each of these three concepts which point to the ground of revelation must be used. [...] The doctrine of revelation is based on a trinitarian interpretation of the divine life and its self-manifestation.[23]

---

23. Paul Tillich, ST1, 156-7.

This passage is quite remarkable. It demonstrates that, even though Tillich begins with the questions of being and reason, his theology is ultimately grounded in the triune God. Correlation is a work of the Spirit to unite form and depth, thereby making the reception of revelation possible. The divine Abyss in God is the hiddenness of God, the unapproachability of the Ultimate. The divine Logos in God is the structure or form, which is incarnate and thus a vital link that makes reason capable of being grasped by revelation. The divine Spirit is the unity of both elements that correlates and unites depth and form. God is the ground of revelation.[24]

This survey of "reason and revelation" confirms my interpretation of Tillich's correlation method as incarnational, christological, and soteriological. But it also adds an important additional description, that Tillich's method is profoundly pneumatological—that is, correlation is based on the divine Spirit as the unity of form and depth. Furthermore, it is trinitarian. Reason (the form) is united with the mystery of revelation (depth) by the divine Spirit in a trinitarian pattern. Tillich's procedure is not to speculate from the questions of being to God, but rather, it is a profound statement that God has reached us in our reason, being, existence, life, and history—liberating, healing, and transfiguring our situation. That is the meaning of love: to reunite the estranged. But to be estranged is to belong essentially to that which one is estranged from. The prodigal son first and always belonged to his father's house, no matter how far he fled. Our reason, being, existence, life, and history belong to a love that passionately reunites us, meets us in our situation, and liberates us to participation in a New Being, which is the reunion of the estranged. To say that God is the answer to the questions implied in being, then, is to say that God is savior, liberator, Father. The correlation method expresses the good news that God truly reaches us in our situation and is the answer to the question of being.

---

24. Karl Barth also recognized the trinitarian pattern of revelation in *Church Dogmatics* I/1, and he constructed a doctrine of the Trinity in connection with the doctrine of revelation accordingly, wherein God is the Revealer, Revelation, and Revealedness. While Tillich does not go so far as to use this pattern to develop a doctrine of the triune God, it is a possible link between the two figures.

The Method of Correlation

This chapter has tried to show that Tillich's controversial method of correlation is not a speculative attempt to derive theological content from the human situation, nor is it a type of natural theology that claims knowledge of God is possible from an analysis of human existence. Instead, the method reflects Tillich's theological commitments, especially his focus on divine grace, the incarnation, the centrality of Christ, and the saving power of the New Being. This correlation is founded on an essential unity between God and humanity, which is why I have called it incarnational. Correlation is a necessary method theologically because God is a love that fervently seeks out the lost, striving to reunite the estranged. There is thus no godless situation; every situation is grasped by the love of God.

Thus, it is also soteriological. The unassumed is the unhealed. Tillich's system articulates how the Christian message has truly reached us in our situation, which necessitates an analysis of the situation. Jesus as the Christ is the manifestation of the essential unity of God and humanity in history. That is the center of Tillich's theology. Jesus is the Christ who brings the New Being. Whatever else might be said about Tillich's method, I hope this chapter has demonstrated that the method is a fruitful attempt at tracing the saving and healing knowledge of God found in the Christian message as the answer to the questions of being that derive from the situation.

Sermon: On Being a Theologian

Tillich preached a three-part sermon to theology students at Union Seminary, articulating what it means to be a theologian. It is instructive for how Tillich understands his own role. The three parts describe a *believing* theologian, a *self-surrendering* theologian, and an *answering* theologian.

In the context of 1 Corinthians 12, Tillich describes theology as a gift of the Spirit. It is this gift, not natural talent, that makes someone a theologian. "The word of knowledge—theology—is spoken *to us* before *we* can say it to others, or even to ourselves. To be a theologian means first of all to be able to *receive* spiritual knowledge."[1] In this sermon, Tillich makes explicit the fact that a theologian does not climb up to revelation through reason, but that we are first spoken to before we speak. Theology is a gift.

Furthermore, theology belongs to a specific community, "the community of those who affirm that Jesus is the Christ.... Theology is a work of the church, precisely because it is a gift of the Divine Spirit."[2] The theologian has been grasped by the Spirit within the church and receives

---

1. Paul Tillich, *The Shaking of the Foundations* (New York: Charles Scribner's Sons, 1948), 119.
2. Ibid., 120.

wisdom and knowledge by grace. However, that does not mean we can overcome our limitations as finite creatures. Indeed, we have no way of knowing for sure that we have truly experienced God. That realization is what Tillich calls the "first condition of theological existence…"[3] It is a realization that leads the theologian to ask "again and again the theological question, the question of an ultimate concern and its manifestations in Jesus as the Christ…"[4]

So, the theologian is not the one who has all the answers but who asks theological questions. As a professor, Tillich was known to emphasize questions in his classroom, both his own questions and those of students, almost more than any answers. And his favorite part of a lecture was the question and answer portion because serious questions arise from the state of being grasped by an ultimate concern. Even doubting questions do not contradict faith. Thus, a believing theologian asks and encourages questions.

In the second sermon, Tillich comments on 1 Corinthians 9, particularly Paul's refrain to be a "servant unto all" and become "all things to all men." Tillich reflects that this is true for the theologian. "The theologian, *in his theology*, must become all things to all men."[5] What this leads to is a theology that accepts its own weakness, acknowledging that weakness and going on in spite of it. It means "restraining ourselves from all fanaticism and theological self-certainty, and by participating—not from the outside, but from the inside—in the weakness of all those to whom we speak as theologians. Our strength is *our weakness*…"[6]

The reason why this is true is that our strength as theologians is not that we possess a message. Rather, we are *possessed by* a message. The role of a theologian is "to point, for our own sake and for the sake of others, to the truth which possess us, but which we do not possess."[7] It is "disastrous" for a theologian to think they have possessed the truth and becomes certain of their theology. There must be a degree of humble weakness in the acknowledgement that we are possessed by a truth we

---

3. Ibid., 121.
4. Ibid.
5. Ibid., 123.
6. Ibid., 125.
7. Ibid.

Sermon: On Being a Theologian

cannot possess in turn. Yet in our weakness, we are possessed by a message, and that is also our strength.

Finally, the third sermon reflects on Paul's famous Mars Hill speech. Here, Tillich reflects on the call to be an *answering* theologian, one who, "in spite of his participation in the weakness and error of all men, is able to answer their questions through the power of his foundation, the New Being in Christ."[8] The role of a theologian is to interpret and explain the reality of New Being in a way that can be understood by those who ask the question of being. Tillich emphasizes, however, that those who ask the question "are not unconscious of the answer…"[9] God is near to everyone, and the very possibility that they might ask the question of being is grounded in the presence of the answer. So, those who ask are in the presence of the answer because God is already near to them.

That refers to Tillich's insistence that God is not an object. "It is bad theology and religious cowardice ever to think that there may be a place where we could look *at* God, as though He were something outside of us to be argued against. Genuine atheism is not humanly possible, for God is nearer to a man than that man is to himself."[10] The idea that an answering theology must *bring* God to those asking questions misunderstands the reality of God. "God is nearer to us than we ourselves."[11] This Augustinian theme is vital to Tillich's theology, and it is why it is wrong to suggest that he has projected the Christian answer from the existential questions. On the contrary, the questions are possible because God is nearer to us than we are to ourselves. We may have a perverted picture of God in need of correcting, but God cannot be an object that is brought to a person. Rather, the reality is that God is present in the questioning and makes it possible.

The task of an answering theologian, then, is to "discover the false gods in the individual soul and in society" in order to challenge them.[12] Tillich refers to the first commandment as "the rock upon which theology stands. There is no synthesis possible between God and idols."[13] In that

---

8. Ibid., 127.
9. Ibid.
10. Ibid., 128.
11. Ibid.
12. Ibid.
13. Ibid., 129.

regard, the theologian "must become an instrument of the Divine Judgement against a distorted world."[14] Finally, that judgment includes the declaration that Jesus is the Christ, which Tillich points out is the aspect of Paul's speech that was finally unacceptable to those in Athens. The theologian must work to remove any of the stumbling blocks that hinder people from hearing this message. That means "we must interpret that paradox, and not throw paradoxical phrases at the minds of people."[15]

The answering theologian's task is to interpret the paradox of Christ in such a way that it can be received by those in the situation today. "We must not impose the heavy burden of wrong stumbling-blocks upon those who ask us questions. But neither must we empty the true paradox of its power."[16] Tillich's unique vocabulary reflects this conviction. He recognized that the language the church used in his time to describe the Christian message had become a stumbling block. Instead of repeating those words, Tillich finds it more useful to speak in a way that meets people where they are in the situation. That is what it means to be an answering theologian.

---

14. Ibid.
15. Ibid.
16. Ibid.

6. Conclusion: What Sort of Theologian is Paul Tillich?

Paul Tillich's theology is surprising, controversial, and complex, but it is also profoundly relatable and pastoral. This book has tried to articulate the core concepts of his thought in a way that makes them more accessible to newcomers. In that spirit, I want to conclude by answering a somewhat odd question: "What sort of theologian is Paul Tillich?" It is necessary to ask this again because it is no longer clear. Tillich has received a reputation for being a purely speculative theologian, an existentialist philosopher, and even an atheist. But as I hope to have shown in this book, these caricatures miss the mark significantly.

A few things should be clarified, however. First, by attempting to answer this question, I do not wish to box Tillich into a fixed mold. His originality forbids any such confinement. But there are categories of his work that I think are worth spelling out because these offer a helpful heuristic lens for new readers. Second, I use *pairs* of terms here to try to grasp at something about his theology that is best articulated as neither fully one thing, or the other. The terms are also not used here as opposites but dialectically, meaning the "and" is not an exclusionary term. This also reflects Tillich's well-known concept of himself as a theologian "on the boundary."

The descriptive pairs are: orthodox and modern, Lutheran and mystical, biblical and philosophical, and mediating and radical. One of the key difficulties in understanding Tillich is how he lives in the boundary spaces between these polarities. For example, those looking for a purely modern theologian will miss his congruence with tradition, and vice versa. So it is through these pairs that I hope to conclude this book. Tillich suggested pairs of polarities in his autobiography, but the pairs considered here are specifically those I found helpful to think about his work. However, they are not exhaustive.

Orthodox and Modern

Tillich is far more orthodox than he appears to be on the surface. Yet, at the same time, Tillich does not merely restate orthodox dogma as if it were timeless and eternal. Orthodoxy, for Tillich, is not a fixed object. The Christian message must be interpreted anew for each generation. Thus, he thoroughly modernizes the Christian message in connection with his analysis of the human situation. So, one way of answering the question of what sort of theologian Tillich is is to suggest that he is orthodox and modern. Yet both terms should be clarified to avoid misunderstanding.

Tillich is orthodox in the sense that he is situated within the Christian tradition and follows the main doctrinal points found in nearly every Christian theology, such as the doctrine of God, the fall and sin, christology, eschatology, and the Protestant doctrine of justification by grace through faith. Yet all of these classical dogmas are radically refreshed by Tillich's approach. That explains his modern tendency. This move is not a betrayal of orthodoxy; instead, it might be argued that a truly orthodox approach to theology is one that embraces somewhat heterodox developments that, as Schleiermacher noted, push orthodoxy forward and eventually become orthodox themselves.[1] Heterodoxy, in this regard, keeps theology mobile. Theology, in other words, is *theologia viatorum*, theology for *pilgrims*. Tillich makes a convincing case that this is what theology has always done when it is at its best. It is only the reactionary or fundamen-

---

1. Schleiermacher, in his *Brief Outline of Theology as a Field of Study*, defines heterodoxy as "Every feature construed in the inclination to keep the body of doctrine mobile and to make room for still other modes of apprehension…" (§203). He argues that both the orthodox and heterodox elements are important, and a true concept of orthodoxy must account for the necessary mobilizing tendencies of heterodoxy.

Conclusion: What Sort of Theologian is Paul Tillich?

talist theologians who insist on equating orthodoxy with the restatement of timeless truths without any concern with the changing human situation. That is what Tillich would call demonic, the absolutizing of finite ideas about God as if they were divine.

Supposedly timeless dogmas from the past are not simply repeated in Tillich. Yet, the spirit, not always the letter, of classic Christian dogma is present and elucidated profoundly by his system. An example is his analysis of the existential situation of estrangement as a re-interpretation of the classic doctrine of the fall. He modernizes this doctrine by avoiding the mythological elements in it that suggest there must be a historical event called the fall, and thus he mitigates the possibility that historical critical research into the Bible or the conclusions of evolutionary science necessarily disrupt Christian faith—yet he retains the theological importance of the fall for soteriological and anthropological insight. And he elevates those insights by reinterpreting the fall in terms relevant to the human situation and in dialogue with existential philosophy. In other words, Tillich has found a way to be at once modern and orthodox. A similar approach might be seen in Tillich's work on nearly every dogmatic question, such as creation, redemption, eternal life, and christology. The spirit of the message is retained while shedding any language he finds inappropriate to the current situation.

Finally, while Tillich's thought contains both orthodox and modern elements, it is not limited by either orthodoxy or modernity. He ultimately strives to transcend both while integrating the spirit of orthodoxy into the language of modernity. It is in that sense that Tillich's theology is orthodox and modern. Thus, I do not mean to imply that Tillich has subjected the Christian faith to the whims of modernity. He is quite critical of modernity at times, just as he is critical of rigidly adhering to the letter of orthodoxy. Rather, he aims to faithfully bear witness to the Christian kerygma in a language that will make sense to modernity, not by subjecting that message to modernity, but by reinterpreting the spirit of the message for the demands of the situation. It is a balancing act, but one that Tillich walks carefully.

LUTHERAN AND MYSTICAL

Another aspect of Tillich's theology is its roots in both the Lutheran tradition, especially in his emphasis on justification by grace through faith, but also his roots in the mystical tradition, particularly the Augustinian. The mystical aspect of Tillich's theology is seen in his frequent evocation (implicitly or explicitly) of Augustine's famous phrase, that "God is nearer to me than I am to myself." Theologically, Tillich makes great use of this insight with his analysis of the human situation. The question implied in being is never without the ground of being that makes it possible to ask the question. An analysis of the situation is possible because of this mystical a priori. Thus, there is no godless place from which an abstract question of being could arise. That leads Tillich to take the human situation seriously as a place where God is already at work, preparing the individual for the answer that can only come by grace. Furthermore, the mystical aspect is apparent in Tillich's doctrine of God as the ground and power of being. This is not only mystical but also profoundly biblical. God is the one in whom we live and move and have our being (Acts 17:28).

But this mysticism is also a type of Lutheran mysticism—as Luther himself was quite mystical—and this adds the dimension of corporeality, i.e., embodiment. Thus, to say Tillich has a mystical dimension does not suggest an escapist or speculative approach. On the contrary, it is a mysticism of the concrete, dealing with real historical bodies under the conditions of finitude. The definition of God as the ground and power of being is a good example. It is a concept of God that fundamentally connects with the human in their actual existence, not an escape from that existence. The power of being is thus "the courage to be," to resist nonbeing. This mysticism is profoundly *embodied*.

Furthermore, the Lutheran emphasis on justification by grace through faith corrects a problematic tendency found in the sort of mysticism that strives for union with God through spiritual works. Instead, for Tillich, this doctrine takes the form of accepting acceptance despite unacceptability.

Besides this emphasis on justification, Tillich is also a theologian of the cross in the classic Lutheran sense. In a sermon, he explains, "There is no human condition into which the divine presence does not penetrate.

Conclusion: What Sort of Theologian is Paul Tillich?

This is what the Cross, the most extreme of all human conditions, tells us."[2] The method of correlation can then be read as a *theologia crucis*; it proclaims the message of the cross, that God has reached us in our estranged condition at its darkest and most god-forsaken, in death and separation. Elsewhere, Tillich reveals that his concept of the "God above God" is rooted in a theology of the cross.[3]

The point in all this is to suggest that locating Tillich within the trajectory of Paul-Augustine-Luther is a far more helpful framework than defining him as a speculative or existential theologian. Whether or not he is successful in adopting this trajectory is another matter. But what is important here is to recognize this link. In many regards, Tillich presupposes this lineage without stating it directly, though it is apparent in the content of his thought.

Biblical and Philosophical

The center of Tillich's system is the message of New Being, but this is basically a re-interpretation (or translation) of 2 Corinthians 5:17, "In Christ, there is a new creation." Thus, Tillich is explicitly Pauline in how he thinks about the Christian message. He states this directly: "If I were asked to sum up the Christian message for our time in two words, I would say with Paul: It is the message of a 'New Creation.'"[4]

Tillich's philosophical orientation often overshadows the fact that he is a biblical theologian. But these need not conflict. Tillich suggests that true biblical faith is at once philosophical. While Tillich does not engage in any lengthy exegesis of biblical texts, his theology is full of biblical allusions and a profound understanding of the overall biblical point of view.

For example, the method of correlation is rooted in Tillich's understanding of the Bible itself. He writes, "The Bible is a document both of the divine self-manifestation and of the way in which human beings have received it."[5] Not even the Bible is pure revelation without also the manifestation of the answer in the context of the human situation, in flesh. As

---

2. Paul Tillich, *The Eternal Now* (New York: Charles Scribner's Sons, 1963), 46.
3. Paul Tillich, *The Courage to Be* (New Haven: Yale University Press, 1952), 188.
4. Paul Tillich, *The New Being* (New York: Charles Scribner's Sons, 1955), 15.
5. Paul Tillich, *Biblical Religion and the Search for Ultimate Reality* (Chicago: The University of Chicago Press, 1955), 4.

Tillich explains, revelation "is always revelation for something and for a group in a definite environment, under unique circumstances."[6] From this point, Tillich argues that the character of the Bible as both revelation and reception necessitates the "confrontation of biblical religion with philosophy."[7] Philosophy analyzes the question of being and the human situation. It is, therefore, impossible to be a biblical theologian without also taking philosophy seriously as a tool for analyzing the human situation. That is the link between philosophy and the Bible in Tillich.

Thus, it is vital for rightly interpreting Tillich that we understand the reason why he is so concerned with philosophy. It is not to establish an argument for the kerygma. Nor is it to extract the Christian message from anthropology or to speculate apart from revelation. Rather, it is because Tillich is a biblical theologian that he takes seriously the way the Bible relates to philosophy and necessitates a continual concern for human reception.

Finally, Tillich rejects the idea that the God of the Bible and the God of the philosophers are irreconcilable: "*Against* Pascal I say: the God of Abraham, Isaac, and Jacob and the God of the philosophers is the same God."[8] That means, for Tillich, there is no conflict between biblical and philosophical theology. That claim informs much of his thought, and it is worth registering to avoid misreading him as purely one or the other, though certainly, it is more common to call him philosophical than it is to call him biblical.

Mediating and Radical

The final pair of descriptions for Tillich is that he is a mediating and radical theologian. Tillich's mediating character is well-known. But it should also be recognized that Tillich is radical even in his mediating approach. Designating his work as mediating can sometimes imply a watered-down approach that tries to make everyone happy, a kind of false peace. Tillich writes, "Wisdom is the acknowledgement of limits… But in saying this, one must protect wisdom against a dangerous distortion of its

---

6. Ibid., 3.
7. Ibid., 5.
8. Ibid., 85.

Conclusion: What Sort of Theologian is Paul Tillich?

meaning—the confusion of wisdom with a philistine avoidance of radical decisions... You cannot find wisdom in those who always avoid radical decisions and adjust themselves to the given situation."[9] Sometimes, mediation is portrayed as a compromise, but that is not what Tillich intends. He makes the radical decisions and, ultimately, works through his mediating approach to transcend both by striving for a new synthesis. He strives to move beyond both liberal and conservative theologies in that regard. His approach always contains a radical striving toward that which can only be fully complete in the eschaton—the unity of heaven and earth.

An instructive example of this is his approach to supernaturalism and naturalism. Tillich critiques the errors of both yet ultimately strives to go beyond their limitations (ST2, 6). Thus, Tillich's system is radically open-ended by design. It anticipates its own surpassing and irrelevance. And that is its greatness. It is self-transcending because of its emphasis on the need for theology to take the changing human situation through culture, politics, and religion seriously. Thus, there is no eternal word objectified by Tillich's system. It is an open-ended approach that has its fulfillment only in the eschaton. Here and now, within the limitations of finitude, all theology is preliminary.

That is Tillich's great humility as a theologian. He recognizes his limitations and actively encourages (even demands) to be surpassed by future theologians attentive to their shifting situations. It is also this aspect of Tillich's work that, to some extent, paved the way for the contextual theologies of liberation that developed in the 1960s. A continual return to the human situation turns theology from a timeless repetition of dogma to an incarnational and deeply human enterprise. For every new generation, the radical message of the New Being must become flesh in the human situation. That means taking seriously the questions implied in being. That is the radical implication behind Tillich's method of correlation. It demands to be done again and again with each new generation. Thus, Tillich's mediating work is never finished, even if he is no longer the one to continue it. It is a radical movement towards synthesis, a synthesis that must again be mediated and overcome by a new synthesis appropriate to each new situation.

---

9. Paul Tillich, *The Eternal Now* (New York: Charles Scribner's Sons, 1963), 168-9.

These pairs of descriptives are presented here to mitigate misreadings of Tillich's theology. Overall, there is much that I find admirable about Tillich's theology. He is, perhaps most of all, a theologian who helps us navigate the ambiguities of life and faith. Theology is often seen as a matter of toeing the line of "correct" doctrine, but Tillich offers a vision that is far more generous and embracing. This includes embracing doubt as a necessary component of faith. When I feel certain doubts about life, God, the church, and myself, I often think about how these doubts are themselves a sign of true faith. And that idea is at once comforting and challenging.

Paul Tillich was a theologian who met people where they are, and his work continues to inspire many today to embrace the risks of faith. For those who, like myself, grew up in a fundamentalist environment where faith was equated with certainty, this journey of embracing the risk of faith is existentially terrifying but also liberating. And on that journey, Tillich can and has been a friend to many. While there are aspects of Tillich's theology that have been superseded by others, there is also much to commend about his work. I hope and pray that this short study of his theology has been informative, but more importantly, I hope it has inspired a deeper faith beyond the false alternatives of certainty and uncertainty. May we all, following Tillich's example, receive and embrace the "courage to be" and go on in spite of our sin, doubt, anxiety, and the ambiguities of life.

Reading Guide

I want to conclude with a brief reading guide before offering a more traditional bibliography. If you're going to read Tillich, you should focus on his *Systematic Theology*. But that work is quite difficult. So you might also start with one of his shorter books, like *Dynamics of Faith, Biblical Religion and the Search for Ultimate Reality,* or *Theology of Culture*. The informal dialogues in *Ultimate Concern* are also quite helpful, as are Tillich's sermons: *The Shaking of the Foundations, The New Being,* and *The Eternal Now*. These loosely correspond to the three volumes of ST. Another important work to study would be Tillich's history lectures, *A History of Christian Thought,* and also Tillich's autobiographies, *On the Boundary* and *My Search for Absolutes*.

But the focus of your reading should be his system. There are two strategies I would like to suggest for reading it. The first approach is to read it straight through normally, ideally reading each volume consecutively. But there is another strategy that was taught to me by my professor at Luther Seminary, Dr. Lois Malcolm. She suggested that I skip the introduction in Volume 1 and first read Tillich's section on "Revelation," then his section on "Reason," and then finally his introduction. From there, the work can be read in order. The goal of this reading is to emphasize the priority Tillich places on revelation and to avoid the misreadings that are far too common, which this book has also argued against. Dr.

Malcolm's advice was helpful for me, and I would recommend it to new readers of Tillich as well. I would also add to her suggestion that special attention should be given to his second volume on Existence and Christ. One might even begin with ST2 and *then* read ST1 in the order she recommended.

Tillich wrote several books beyond those already mentioned that are well worth reading, depending on your interest. The works I would consider essential include *The Courage to Be, What is Religion?, Christianity and the Encounter of World Religions,* and *The Protestant Era.* But in the bibliography that follows, I will list all of the English texts I am aware of.

My final advice for reading Tillich is to remember Tillich's context and goals. To grasp these, I would suggest that you should read as much of his work as you can before making critical judgments. Tillich is a profoundly interconnected thinker, and so if you do not always understand something, there is a good chance he will raise the issue in another context where it makes more sense to you. That is a general strategy I have adopted for reading difficult figures: do not worry about understanding every detail; understand what you can and use that to help you with the more difficult issues.

As far as secondary literature is concerned, the books I found most helpful were Christian Danz's *The Theology of Paul Tillich,* Daniel J. Peterson's *Tillich,* Donald W. Musser and Joseph L. Price's *Tillich,* Russell Re Manning, ed., *The Cambridge Companion to Paul Tillich,* and Langdon Gilkey's *Gilkey on Tillich.* I would also highly recommend Wilhelm and Marion Pauck's biography of Tillich.

Bibliography

Works by Paul Tillich (chronological):

Tillich, Paul, trans. H. Richard Niebuhr, *The Religious Situation* (New York: Henry Holt and Co., 1931).
—— *The Interpretation of History,* trans. N. A. Rasetzki and Elsa L. Talmey (New York: Charles Scribner's Sons, 1936).
—— *The Protestant Era,* trans. James Luther Adams (Chicago: University of Chicago Press, 1948).
—— *The Shaking of the Foundations* (New York: Charles Scribner's Sons, 1948).
—— *Systematic Theology,* three volumes (Chicago: University of Chicago Press, 1951, 1957, 1963).
—— *The Courage to Be* (New Haven: Yale University Press, 1952).
—— *Love, Power, and Justice: Ontological Analysis & Ethical Applications* (New York: Oxford University Press, 1954).
—— *The New Being* (New York: Charles Scribner's Sons, 1955).
—— *Biblical Religion and the Search for Ultimate Reality* (Chicago: University of Chicago Press, 1955).
—— *The Eternal Now* (New York: Charles Scribner's Sons, 1956).
—— "Autobiographical Reflections" and "Reply to Interpretation and Criticism" in Charles W. Kegley and Robert W. Bretall, eds., *The Theology of Paul Tillich* (New York: The Macmillan Company, 1956).
—— *Dynamics of Faith* (New York: Harper & Row, 1957).
—— *Theology of Culture* (London: Oxford University Press, 1959).
—— *Christianity and the Encounter of the World Religions* (New York: Columbia University Press, 1963).
—— *Ultimate Concern: Tillich in Dialogue,* ed. D. Mackenzie Brown (New York: Harper & Row, 1965).
—— *The World Situation* (Philadelphia: Fortress Press, 1965).
—— *On the Boundary: An Autobiographical Sketch* (New York: Charles Scribner's Sons, 1966).
—— *The Future of Religions,* ed. Jerald C. Brauer (New York: Harper & Row, 1966).
—— *My Search for Absolutes* (New York: Simon and Schuster, 1967).
—— *A History of Christian Thought,* ed. Carl E. Braaten (New York: Simon and Schuster, 1968).
—— *What is Religion?,* ed. James Luther Adams (New York: Harper & Row, 1969).
—— *My Travel Diary: 1936* (New York: Harper & Row, 1970).
—— *Political Expectations,* ed. James Luther Adams (New York: Harper & Row Publishers, 1971).
—— *Mysticism and Guilt-Consciousness in Schelling's Philosophical Development,* trans. Victor Nuovo (Lewisburg: Bucknell University Press, 1974).
—— *The Construction of the History of Religion in Schelling's Positive Philosophy: Its Pressupositions and Principles,* trans. Victor Nuovo (Lewisburg: Bucknell University Press, 1974).

Bibliography

—— *The Socialist Decision,* trans. Franklin Sherman (New York: Harper & Row Publishers, 1977).

—— *The System of the Sciences according to Objects and Methods,* trans. Paul Wiebe (Lewisburg, PA: Bucknell University Press, 1981).

—— *The Meaning of Health,* ed. Perry LeFevre (Chicago: Exploration Press, 1984).

—— *The Essential Tillich: An Anthology of the Writings of Paul Tillich,* ed. Forrest Church (New York: Macmillan Publishing Company, 1987).

—— *The Spiritual Situation and Our Technical Society,* ed. J. Mark Thomas (Macon, GA: Mercer University Press, 1988).

—— *On Art and Architecture,* ed. John and Jane Dillenberger (New York: Crossroad, 1989).

—— "Philosophical Writings" in *Main Works / Hauptwerke,* volume one, ed. Carl Heinz Ratschow (Berlin/New York: De Gruyter, 1989).

—— *The Theology of Peace,* ed. Ronald H. Stone (Louisville: Westminster/John Knox, 1990).

—— *The Irrelevance and Relevance of the Christian Message,* ed. A Durwood Foster (Pilgrims Press, 1996; reprint Eugene, OR: Wipf & Stock, 2007).

—— *Against the Third Reich: Paul Tillich's Wartime Addresses to Nazi Germany,* trans. Matthew Lon Weaver, ed. Ronald H. Stone and Matthew Lon Weaver (Louisville: Westminster John Knox Press, 1998).

—— *The Ground of Being: Neglected Essays of Paul Tillich,* ed. Robert M. Price (Mindvendor Publications, 2015).

Secondary sources (alphabetical):

Adams, James Luther, *Paul Tillich's Philosophy of Culture, Science & Religion* (Washington: University Press of America, 1982).

Adams, James Luther, Wilhelm Pauck, Roger Lincoln Shinn, eds., *The Thought of Paul Tillich* (San Francisco: Harper & Row, 1985).

Braaten, Carl E., "Paul Tillich's Message for Our Time" in *Anglican Theological Review* 72:1 (1990), 16-25.

Bulman, Raymond F. and Frederick J. Parrella, ed., *Paul Tillich: A New Catholic Assessment* (Collegeville, MN: The Liturgical Press, 1994).

Clayton, John Powell, *The Concept of Correlation: Paul Tillich and the Possibility of a Mediating Theology* (Berlin: Walter de Gruyter, 1980).

Cooper, John Charles, *The "Spiritual Presence" in the Theology of Paul Tillich: Tillich's Use of St. Paul* (Macon, GA: Mercer University Press, 1997).

Danz, Christian, *The Theology of Paul Tillich: Contexts and Key Issues* (Macon, GA: Mercer University Press, 2024).

Donnelly, Brian, *The Socialist Emigre: Marxism and the Later Tillich* (Macon, GA: Mercer University Press, 2003).

Ferré, F. S. Nels, et. al., *Paul Tillich: Retrospect and Future* (Nashville: Abingdon Press, 1966).

Gilkey, Langdon, *Gilkey on Tillich* (New York: Crossroad, 1990).

Hamilton, Kenneth, *The System and the Gospel: A Critique of Paul Tillich* (New York: The Macmillan Company, 1963).

Hopper, David, *Tillich: A Theological Portrait* (Philadelphia: J. B. Lippincott, 1968).

Irwin, Alexander C., *Eros Toward the World: Paul Tillich and the Theology of the Erotic* (Minneapolis: Fortress Press, 1991).

Bibliography

Jennings, Brach S., "The Courage to Be: Paul Tillich's Existentialist Theology of the Cross in Relation to Martin Luther" in *Dialog* 25 (2018), 211-218.

Johnson, Wayne G., *Theological Method in Luther and Tillich: Law-Gospel and Correlation* (Washington: University Press of America, 1981).

Kegley, Charles W. and Robert W. Bretall, *The Theology of Paul Tillich* (New York: The Macmillan Company, 1956).

Kelsey, David H., *The Fabric of Paul Tillich's Theology* (New Haven: Yale University Press, 1967).

Malcom, Lois, "Mystical and Prophetic" in *Bulletin of the North American Paul Tillich Society*, 32-4 (Fall 2006), 9-14.

Manning, Russell Re, ed., *The Cambridge Companion to Paul Tillich* (Cambridge University Press, 2009).

Manning, Russell Re, ed., *Retrieving the Radical Tillich: His Legacy and Contemporary Importance* (New York: Palgrave Macmillan, 2015).

Manning, Russell Re and Samuel Shearn, ed., *Returning to Tillich* (Berlin: Walter de Gruyter, 2018).

Mahan, Wayne W., *Tillich's System* (San Antonio, Trinity University Press, 1974).

Martin, Bernard, *The Existentialist Theology of Paul Tillich* (New York: Bookman Associates, 1963).

May, Rollo, *Paulus: A Personal Portrait of Paul Tillich* (New York: Harper & Row, 1973).

McKelway, Alexander J., *The Systematic Theology of Paul Tillich: A Review and Analysis* (Richmond: John Knox Press, 1964).

Musser, Donald W. and Joseph L. Price, *Tillich* (Nashville: Abingdon Press, 2010).

Nuovo, Victor, *Visionary Science: A Translation of Tillich's "On the Idea of a Theology of Culture" with an Interpretive Essay* (Detroit: Wayne State University Press, 1987).

O'Neill, Andrew, *Tillich: A Guide for the Perplexed* (New York: T&T Clark, 2008).

Pomeroy, Richard M., *Paul Tillich: A Theology for the 21st Century* (San Jose: Writer's Showcase, 2002).

Stone, Ronald H., *Paul Tillich's Radical Social Thought* (Washington: University Press of America, 1986).

Thomas, J. Heywood, *Paul Tillich* (Richmond: John Knox Press, 1965).

Tillich, Hannah, *From Time to Time* (New York: Stein and Day, 1973).

Peterson, Daniel J., *Tillich: A Brief Overview of the Life and Writings of Paul Tillich* (Minneapolis: Lutheran University Press, 2013).

Stenger, Mary Ann and Ronald H. Stone, *Dialogues of Paul Tillich* (Mercer University Press, 2002).

Wariboko, Nimi and Amos Yong, ed., *Paul Tillich and Pentecostal Theology: Spiritual Presence and Spiritual Power* (Bloomington: Indiana University Press, 2015).

Yip, Francis Ching-Wah, *Capitalism as Religion?: A Study of Paul Tillich's Interpretation of Modernity* (Cambridge: Harvard University Press, 2010).

www.ingramcontent.com/pod-product-compliance
Lightning Source LLC
Chambersburg PA
CBHW070057080526
44586CB00013B/1098